Close Up

A Critical Introduction to Film

Preliminary Edition

Craig Padawer
Westchester Community College

Kendall Hunt
publishing company

Kendall Hunt
publishing company

www.kendallhunt.com
Send all inquiries to:
4050 Westmark Drive
Dubuque, IA 52004-1840

Printed in the United States of America
10 9 8 7 6 5 4 3 2 1

Contents

CHAPTER 1

Narrative

What Is Narrative?

A narrative is a series of events linked together by causality, chronology, and spatial relationships. Events alone do not constitute a narrative. They need to be placed into context and linked together by time, space, and cause. Let's take as an example the following events from Milos Forman's *One Flew over the Cuckoo's Nest*.

- The Chief smothers McMurphy with a pillow
- McMurphy tries to strangle Nurse Ratched
- Billy commits suicide
- McMurphy undergoes a lobotomy
- Billy sleeps with Candy

Listed in this way, the events don't tell us much. In fact, they provide more questions than answers. First of all, questions of character motivation arise. Why does the Chief smother McMurphy? What causes Billy to commit suicide? Why does McMurphy try to strangle Nurse Ratched? Are the characters all just irrational?

Without a narrative structure to establish the connections between these events, we would simply have random acts committed by inscrutable individuals. It would be impossible for us to make sense of, and thus care about, either the characters or the story. Second, the list of occurrences raises disturbing questions about the nature of the world portrayed in the film. The first item on the list has the Chief smothering McMurphy, but after that, McMurphy tries to strangle Nurse Ratched. Similarly, Billy commits suicide and then sleeps with Candy. Perhaps this is a horror film and both Billy and McMurphy have returned from the dead—Billy in order to lose his virginity, and McMurphy in order to settle some old score with Nurse Ratched. Or maybe *One Flew over the Cuckoo's Nest* is a thriller in which Billy fakes his own suicide, and in which McMurphy somehow survives the Chief's attempt on his life and then attacks Nurse Ratched because he believes she ordered the Chief to try to kill him.

If you find neither of these explanations very plausible, you're justified in your suspicion. Forman's film is neither a zombie flick nor a sleight-of-hand mystery. The confusion stems from the fact that three key ingredients are missing from the brief list of events given above.

The first missing ingredient is causality. **Causality** is the process by which one event leads to or influences another. In *One Flew over the Cuckoo's Nest (1975)*, Nurse Ratched threatens to tell Billy's mother that he's slept with Candy (**1.1**). As a result, Billy commits suicide (**1.2**). Enraged by what Ratched has done (**1.3**), McMurphy attacks her (**1.4**). He is then forcibly restrained and, later, given a lobotomy that leaves him in a vegetative state. Unable to bear the sight of McMurphy in this condition (**1.6**), the Chief smothers him with a pillow (**1.7** and **1.8**). Here we have a chain in which each event tragically causes the next. The motives of the characters must be established through action and dialogue so that the causal relationships between events are apparent to viewers. In this case, we have learned through previous action and dialogue that Nurse Ratched is an authoritarian who takes pleasure in controlling and humiliating her patients, that McMurphy is a rebellious non-conformist set on undermining Ratched's authority, and that Billy is a timid stutterer, longing to experience life but intimidated by a repressive mother.

The second ingredient necessary to our narrative is **chronology**, or the order in which the events occur in time. Chronology is crucial to establishing the cause

1.1
Nurse Ratched threatens to tell Billy's mother what he's done in *One Flew over the Cuckoo's Nest*.

1.2
Billy's suicide.

1.3
McMurphy grows enraged . . .

1.4
. . . and attacks Ratched.

1.5
A continuity error: the hat is back on.

1.6
McMurphy after his lobotomy.

1.7
The Chief . . .

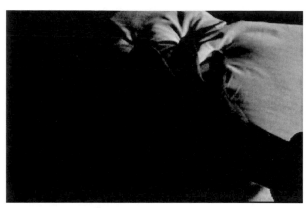

1.8
. . . smothers McMurphy.

and effect relationship between the events. For example, if Billy committed suicide after McMurphy attacked Nurse Ratched, his suicide could not have caused the attack. Similarly, we need to know that McMurphy has been reduced to a vegetative state by the lobotomy in order to understand why his friend, the Chief, smothers him at the end of the film. Without knowing the order in which the events occur, a viewer is unable to determine the causal relationships. Altering the chronological order of the events alters the causal relationships and—as we saw in our zombie example—creates a profoundly different narrative.

Finally, a narrative unfolds not only over time, but also in space. Billy's suicide would have no effect on McMurphy if the two men did not coexist in the common space of the mental institution. This space is subdivided into wards, offices, and treatment rooms. In addition, some of the narrative action occurs outside the institution. The film's events make sense only in the context of these various spaces and the ways in which the characters move through them—that is, in terms of their **spatial relationships**. Billy is able to take his own life only because he is left alone in one of the doctors' offices. McMurphy, whose primary goal at this point in the film is to escape with the Chief, is down the hall in the day room, about to climb out an open window (**1.3**), when one of the nurses discovers Billy's body and screams. McMurphy goes back to see what has happened, and in doing so he seals his fate.

The maintaining of spatial, temporal and causal relationships in a film is referred to as **continuity**. When a movie fails to maintain continuity, the effect can be distracting to viewers, shattering the illusion of reality that the film is seeking maintain. Such an error occurs in **1.4** and **1.5**, where the action fails to unfold logically in time and space. Notice that the hat McMurphy wears (**1.3**) has fallenoff during his struggle with Nurse Ratched (**1.4**). Inexplicably, the hat is back on McMurphy's head in the next shot (**1.5**).

Elements of Narrative

Now that we have a sense of what a narrative is, let's take a look at its basic elements.

Setting is the time and place in which the events of the narrative occur. Time is an important element of setting and should not be overlooked. Places are not static; the New York City of *Gangs of New York* (2002), which is set in 1863, looks very different from the New York City of *Taxi Driver* (1976), which is set in the early 1970s. Architecture, style of dress, and modes of transportation all changed drastically during the hundred-year period between the two narratives. Sometimes changes occur more swiftly. In a matter of minutes, the events of 9/11 permanently altered the New York City skyline. Even the natural landscape may change significantly over time, as is evidenced by photographs of Mount Saint Helens before and after its eruption (**1.9**). *Back to the Future* (1985) takes place in one location—Hill Valley, California—during two different times, 1985 and 1955. Here the changes wrought by time become a key plot element. We will discuss setting in greater detail in Chapter 2.

Story is the totality of dramatic events in the order in which they originally occurred, including events actually presented in the film and those that are surmised or assumed by the audience. In *It Happened One Night* (1934), we see Ellie dive off her father's yacht and swim away. When she appears at the bus station in the next scene, she is dry and dressed in different clothes. We don't actually see her emerge from the water, buy new clothes, dry off, and change, but we surmise these events; they are part of the story. Similarly, we don't see Charley actually get murdered by Johnny Friendly's crew in *On the Waterfront* (1954). We see the results of the murder—we see Terry discover his brother's bullet-riddled body hanging from a longshoreman's hook—and we infer what has transpired.

1.9
Photos of Mount Saint Helens before and after its eruption on May 18, 1980.

Plot differs from story in that it consists of the story material as it has been structured and arranged by the storyteller. Charley's murder is part of the story in *On the Waterfront*, but not part of the plot because Elia Kazan chose to leave that scene out of the film. Plot often manipulates chronology or withholds information for dramatic purposes. In Alfred Hitchcock's *Vertigo* (1958), Gavin Elstir is waiting for Judy at the top of the tower with the body of his murdered wife, but the plot initially withholds this information from the audience, revealing it later in a flashback.

Diegesis refers to the world of the story and anything that is a part of that world. If a character is listening to a song playing on the radio, the song is **diegetic**. However, if the song is part of the soundtrack of the film and cannot be heard by the characters, it is **non-diegetic**. Non-diegetic elements that appear in a film are considered to be part of the plot but not part of the story. For example, film credits are nondiegetic and therefore part of a film's plot but not part of its story. The same is true of non-diegetic visual elements such as the shot of sheep (**1.10**) that precedes the shot of the workers emerging from the subway (**1.11**) in Charlie Chaplin's *Modern Times* (1936). The non-diegetic shot creates a comparison between the workers and the sheep. It is part of the plot because it appears onscreen, but it is intrusive; it sticks out precisely because it is not part of the world of the story.

Characters are the individuals who populate the story. They are typically human, but not always. The main character in *A.I* (2001). is a robot boy who, like Pinocchio, wants to be human; most of the characters in Wes Andersen's *The Fantastic Mr. Fox* (2009) are wild animals; and the characters in *Toy Story* (1995) are, well, toys. When nonhuman characters appear in a story, they are often **anthropomorphized**—that is, given human attributes. The **protagonist** is the main character of the story, the character around whom the action revolves and with whom the audience typically identifies. The **antagonist** is the character who opposes the protagonist. In *No Country for Old Men* (2007), Llewelyn Moss (Josh Brolin) is the protagonist, while the pathological hit man Anton Chigurh (Javier Bardem) is the film's antagonist. Characters may be **flat** (one dimensional) or **round** (complex, multilayered). **Dynamic** characters are those who change during the course of the film, while **static** characters remain the same.

As the terms "protagonist" and "antagonist" imply, at the center of most stories lies a **conflict**, a struggle between opposing forces. Conflicts may be **external** or **internal**—many films contain both types of conflicts. Often the protagonist struggles against an external force in the form of an antagonist while at the same time struggling with his own shortcomings. In *On the Waterfront*, the external

1.10
A non-diegetic shot of sheep . . .

1.11
. . . is juxtaposed with one of workers in Chaplin's *Modern Times* (1936).

conflict is between Terry and Johnny Friendly, but the internal conflict is between Terry and his conscience.

The conflict is precipitated by a dramatic crisis, which arises when the status quo or established order at the beginning of the film is disturbed by one or more **disordering events**. This established order, sometimes referred to as the film's **opening balance**, should not be confused with a state of perfection or bliss. During the opening balance, the protagonist is not necessarily content but is in a state of stasis (motionlessness). In *Casablanca* (1942), Rick Blaine is not exactly a happy person when we meet him at the beginning of the film (he is cynical, bitter, and lonely), but he has made a life for himself in Casablanca—he has established a routine, found a balance. That balance is disrupted by the appearance of Ilsa and her husband at Rick's Café Américain. The same goes for Terry in *On the Waterfront*. At the beginning of the film, he has given up on his dreams and harbors bitter resentments, but he has carved out a meager life for himself on the waterfront. Two disordering events—Joey Doyle's murder and the appearance of Edie—precipitate the dramatic crisis that propels Terry to change. In the case of *Out of the Past* (1947), the opening balance does reflect the protagonist's sense of harmony and contentment. Jeff is truly happy with Ann, although the shadow of his undisclosed past hangs over them. The appearance of Joe in Bridgeport disrupts both the opening balance and Jeff's happiness.

Conflict generates plot. Plot contains several elements: exposition, rising action, climax, falling action, and resolution or dénouement. **Exposition** refers to the setup of the story; it conveys the circumstances of the situation and the backgrounds of the relevant characters, and it establishes the conflict. In a "classical" Hollywood narrative (the type of narrative that has dominated Hollywood since the early days of cinema), **rising action** usually occupies the bulk of the film and consists of a pattern of increasingly intense action. The protagonist encounters obstacles, attempts to overcome them, and suffers setbacks. The rising action leads to the film's **climax**, the moment of greatest intensity or tension. The conflict between the protagonist and the antagonist comes to a head in the climax and an outcome is determined. Following the climax, the action diminishes in intensity—it falls off (**falling action**). The French term **dénouement** translates roughly as "untying the knot." In a classical film's denouement, the complications generated by the conflict are resolved and order is restored. The classical (or conventional) narrative paradigm can be illustrated by the diagram below (**1.12**).

The diagram is a bit of an oversimplification. Exposition, for example, is often distributed over the course of a film as information about characters and events is revealed later in the story. One of the most well-known examples of "late exposition"

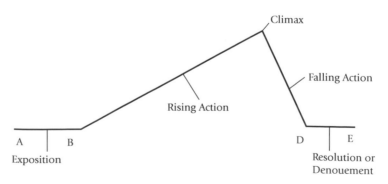

1.12
Classical narrative structure.

occurs in *The Empire Strikes Back* (1980) when, very late in the film, Darth Vader reveals to Luke that he is his father.

You will also note that conventional narrative structure as it is depicted in this
model is linear. The story proceeds along a single line and events unfold in chronological order. But even classical Hollywood films sometimes depart from this structure. The linear narrative structure of *Casablanca*, for example, is disrupted by the
flashback sequence chronicling the love affair between Rick and Ilsa in Paris. The
film noirs of the 1940s and 1950s frequently employed flashbacks. *Double Indemnity* (1944) consists of a present tense frame story in which a wounded Walter Neff
narrates the main story into a Dictaphone in the form of a long flashback. In both
of these cases, the linear nature of the story is left primarily intact. In *Citizen Kane*
(1941), however, Orson Welles uses five different flashback sequences and decon-
structs the story to such a great degree that the film becomes a meditation on the
elusive and illusory nature of narrative itself—a reflection on the difficulty, perhaps
even the impossibility, of telling a story. More recently, filmmakers such as Quentin Tarantino have experimented with plot structures that undermine the temporal
coherence of their films. In *Pulp Fiction* (1994), Tarantino develops several plot
strands simultaneously and presents viewers with sequences that sometimes overlap and often do not occur in chronological order. The viewer must construct the
linear narrative for herself out of the pieces provided by the filmmaker. Influenced
by Tarantino's use of multiple plot strands, Alejandro González Iñárritu employs a
narrative structure that looks very different than the one depicted in our diagram
of the classical paradigm. *Amores Perros* (2000) employs three different narrative
strands that briefly converge and then diverge again (**1.13**).

As a rule, classical narratives tend to be tightly structured and focused on a
single protagonist, their plots driven by character psychology, strong causal relationships, and clear resolutions. Extraneous story material is edited out of the
plot, time is compressed, and an illusion of objectivity is created. But, as we will
see in later chapters, this is not the only way to tell a story. Soviet montage, the
French New Wave, Italian neorealism, and filmmakers of both the avant-garde
and the commercial variety have bent, broken, or simply ignored the "rules" of

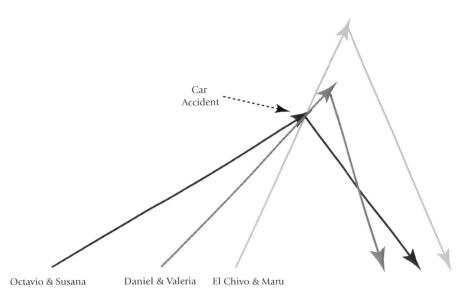

Car
Accident

Octavio & Susana   Daniel & Valeria   El Chivo & Maru

1.13
Plot structure of *Amores Perros (2000)*.

conventional narrative for as long as those rules have been around. In Luis Buñuel's *Un Chien Andalou* (1928), the causal relationships between events are obscure or nonexistent, temporal and spatial relationships are dissolved, character psychology no longer seems to motivate behavior or drive events, and objective reality gives way to the illogical discontinuity of dreams. The same could be said of David Lynch's *Mulholland Drive* (2001)—or, for that matter, Jean-Luc Godard's *Breathless* (1960). Films such as *Un chien andalou* and *Mulholland Drive* are surrealist in style and sensibility—they attempt to capture the irrational logic of the unconscious. But realist films—films that attempt to portray life "as it is," without overdramatizing events—also dispense with classical narrative structure. A plot diagram of Jim Jarmusch's *Broken Flowers* (2005) would look more like a gently undulating line than like a classical narrative pyramid with a dramatic climax at its apex.

CHAPTER 2

Cinematography

The process by which moving images are recorded on film is referred to as **cinematography**. The cinematographer determines the look of a film through the use of camerawork, lenses, film stock, lighting, filters, and in some cases special effects. While cinematography has much in common with still photography, it differs from it in some very important ways, not the least of which is the fact that the images captured by the cinematographer are moving.

The Frame

The first motion pictures evolved out of the serial photography of Eadweard Muybridge (1830–1904). Muybridge executed his first serial photographs in 1872. In order to settle a bet on whether a galloping horse lifted all four hooves off the ground at once, he devised a method of photographing a horse in motion, using first twelve and later twenty-four cameras triggered one after another as the horse came down the track (**2.1**).

2.1
Eadward Muybridge's sequential photographs of a galloping horse.

These serial photographs, which recorded the horse's motion in individual frames, inspired inventors such as Etienne-Jules Marey, Emile Reynaud, Hannibal Goodwin, and Augustin Le Prince to develop their own mechanisms for capturing motion in the form of multiple images and in some cases for projecting those images. However, it wasn't until 1891 when Thomas Alva Edison and his assistant W. K. L. Dickson unveiled their Kinetograph camera and Kinetoscope viewer that motion pictures were truly born. The Edison invention employed strips of Eastman Kodak film cut to a width of approximately 35 millimeters with sprocket holes punched in the bottom edge so that the film could be guided through the machine.

In a motion picture camera, the film advances through the camera housing, pausing briefly before the aperture, where that section of film is exposed to light entering through the camera lens. Each exposure constitutes a **frame**. A film projector essentially reverses the camera process. The projector contains a light source inside it.

2.2
Use of onscreen and
offscreen space . . .

2.3
. . . in *The Maltese
Falcon* (1941).

When a film is projected, a shutter inside the projector breaks the light beam twice for each frame. The result is an illusion in which the individual frames appear to the viewer as a continuous moving image. Most films are recorded and projected at twenty-four frames per second, although early films ran at a slower rate, in some cases sixteen or twenty frames per second. A modern feature film may contain over 170,000 frames.

The term "frame" also refers to the rectangular boundary of the cinematic image as it appears on screen. The dimensions of the frame will vary depending upon the **aspect ratio** of the film. Most early silent films had an aspect ratio of 1.33:1. With the advent of sound in the late 1920s, the aspect ratio of some films changed to 1.17:1, resulting in a nearly square frame in order to allow the filmstrip to accommodate the sound track. By the early 1930s most films were being printed in an actual aspect ratio of 1.375:1, which is sometimes referred to as **Academy ratio** or Academy format; this ratio is still commonly, and inaccurately, designated as 1.33:1. This aspect ratio remained the standard for films made prior to the 1950s, at which point widescreen formats were introduced. The two most common widescreen aspect ratios are 1.85:1 and 2.40:1 (formerly 2.35:1). In order to create a widescreen image, the top and bottom portion of the frame are blacked out or **masked** either during shooting or during screening.

The frame's boundaries separate **onscreen space** (what we see) from **offscreen space** (what we don't see). The director, in consultation with the cinematographer, decides what to include in the frame and how to include it. By manipulating the frame, filmmakers can create coherent spatial relationships, withhold or reveal information, or shock the viewer. If a character looks offscreen in one shot and the film then cuts to another shot, viewers will connect the two and conclude that the second shot represents what the character is seeing (this is known as an **eyeline match** and will be discussed further in Chapter 4). Onscreen and offscreen space can also be used to withhold or reveal information and to startle the viewer. In *The Maltese Falcon* (1941), Miles Archer appears onscreen smiling in the direction of the camera (**2.2**). His smile then turns to a look of fear as a hand holding a gun appears in the frame (**2.3**). Here framing is used to achieve two goals: the sudden appearance of the gun from offscreen takes the viewer by surprise, while the camera position conceals the identity of Archer's killer from the audience.

Shots and Scenes

A **shot** is one uninterrupted run of the camera resulting in a continuous image. Put another way, a shot consists of the image produced from the time the camera starts running until the time it stops. The very earliest films, such as those of Auguste (1862–1954) and Louis (1864–1948) Lumière, each consisted of a single unedited shot or take—sometimes referred to as a **sequence shot**—approximately one minute in length. As film technology advanced, shot counts increased. These days, it is not unusual for a two-hour film to contain 2000 or more shots.

Once the camera is stopped—in order to move it to a new position, for example—the shot is completed and what follows is a new shot. A conversation between two characters might begin with a long shot that includes both actors, cut to a second shot consisting of a close-up of Actor A, and then go to a close-up of Actor B for a total of three separate shots. This is a simplification, of course. Often a scene such as the one described will consist of far more than three shots and will include shots from a range of distances and positions. We will examine this topic more closely in Chapter 4, when we discuss editing.

It should also be noted that our definition of a shot holds true whether the camera is stationary or in motion. Unlike still photography, which produces static

2.4
Steve Buscemi in *Fargo*
(1996).

images, cinema captures figures and objects in motion. In addition, the cinematic frame—the rectangular border that defines the limits of the image—has the potential to become mobile if the camera itself is in motion during filming. Imagine the scene we just described filmed with a highly mobile camera. In that case, we might begin with a long shot of the characters seated at a table talking. The camera might then slowly move in on Actor A, pausing for a close-up, then draw back and swing around to turn its attention to Actor B, moving in for another close-up. All this time the camera would be running. The result would be a single, uninterrupted shot rather than the three separate shots described in our previous example.

A **scene** is a narrative unit usually composed of one or more shots. A scene is confined to a single period of time and typically takes place in one location. The exceptions are scenes that employ **crosscutting** to depict two or more actions occurring at the same time but in different places (also known as **parallel action**). In *Fargo* (1996), crosscutting is used to depict the telephone conversation between Carl Showalter (Steve Buscemi) and Jerry Lundegaard (William H. Macy). Carl is calling from a payphone in a bar (**2.4**), while Jerry is speaking from his living room (**2.5**). Despite the fact that the events unfold in two different locations, they occur at the same time and thus constitute a single scene. Their simultaneity is indicated by the alternating shots of Jerry and Carl. (Both crosscutting and scene construction will be discussed further in Chapter 4.)

2.5
William H. Macy in
Fargo.

Camera Distance

When we speak of **camera distance**, we are really speaking of the perceived distance between the camera and the subject. The actual distance between the camera and the subject is often impossible to gauge because it depends on the lens being used. For example, a shot in which the subject's face fills the frame may be produced by placing the camera in close proximity to the subject or by using a zoom lens from a distance. In either case, the viewer will be left with the impression or the perception of being in proximity to the subject.

The terminology used to describe camera distances is not exact. An entire range of shots falls under the category of medium shots, for example. In addition, shots are often not static. The subject, the camera, or both, may move. What starts off as one type of shot may become another, as in the case of the shot from *Kill Bill: Vol. 2* (2004). As Uma Thurman walks toward the doorway, the perceived distance between her and the camera changes. What was technically a medium long shot (**2.6**) becomes a long shot (**2.7**). In a case like this, it is not possible to accurately classify the shot with a

2.6
Kill Bill: Vol. 2 (2004).

2.7
Kill Bill: Vol. 2.

single term. For this reason, it's best to think of these terms as approximations and use them accordingly in your writing. If the majority of a shot falls into a particular category, such as a long shot, then classify it as such even though there may be moments in which the shot falls outside that criterion.

An **extreme long shot** is one in which the camera is placed at a great distance from the subject, whether that subject is a human figure or an element of the landscape. If a human figure is included in the shot, it is usually dwarfed by the surrounding environment. The shot is often used to emphasize the insignificance or vulnerability of characters and is particularly effective in portraying man's struggle with the elements. *Lawrence of Arabia* (1962) emphasizes the scorching vastness of the desert through the use of extreme long shots that reduce the human figure to a dot on the horizon (**2.8**). The shot is used frequently in Westerns, such as John Ford's *The Searchers* (1956) (**2.9**), because it showcases both the beauty and the desolation of the landscape and captures the frailty of human life in a harsh, lawless,

2.8
Extreme long shot: a lone camel rider crosses the vast desert in *Lawrence of Arabia* (1962).

2.9
In this extreme long shot from *The Searchers* (1956), the riders are dwarfed by the towering rock formations.

2.10
An interior extreme long shot from *Citizen Kane* (1941) portrays Charles Foster Kane as dwarfed by his own possessions.

and frequently hostile environment. Interior extreme long shots are rare because of the distance required, but when they are used they can be very effective in conveying loneliness and isolation as they do in *Citizen Kane*, where Charles Foster Kane appears to wander like a lost child through the vast empty spaces of Xanadu (**2.10**).

Because extreme long shots are taken from a great distance, they are well suited for establishing shots. An establishing shot serves as a transition between scenes by introducing the location in which the subsequent action will occur. In *The Maltese Falcon*, an extreme long shot of the Golden Gate Bridge with the superimposed title "San Francisco" establishes the story's setting (**2.11**).

2.11
An extreme long shot with superimposed title used to establish location in *The Maltese Falcon* (1941).

2.12
A full shot from *Bringing Up Baby* (1938).

The **long shot** includes a wide range of camera distances. Typically it refers to a shot in which the entire human form is visible in the frame and in which some portion of the setting is apparent. When the human figure nearly fills the frame, the long shot is referred to as a **full shot**. A full shot from *Bringing Up Baby* (1938) (**2.12**) reveals the full bodies of the actors and just a portion of the setting. However, when the location becomes more crucial to the action, a shot from a greater distance may be required to reveal more of the setting. In this long shot from *Jaws* (1975) (**2.13**), the frame height is more than twice that of the human figure in order to accommodate the boat. Visually, long shots tend to coincide with what we might expect to see on stage in a live theater production.

2.13
A long shot from *Jaws* (1975).

2.14
A shot/reverse-shot combination . . .

2.15
. . . in Marcel Carné's *Port of Shadows* (1938).

Medium shots show the figure from the ankle, knees, or waist up. Shots from the ankles or knees up may also sometimes be referred to as **medium long shots**. A medium or medium long shot may also be designated by the number of figures in it, as in a **two-shot** or a three-shot. Anything over a three-shot usually becomes a full shot because of the distance required to fit the figures in the frame. An **over-the-shoulder shot** is a medium shot (usually a two-shot) used most commonly in a shot/reverse-shot combination to portray a conversation between characters as in *Port of Shadows* (1938) (**2.14** and **2.15**).

A **close-up** shows little or none of the scene's surrounding and concentrates on a single object that nearly fills the frame. Typically the subject of the close-up is the human face, but it may also be another part of the human body, or it may be an object to which the director wishes to draw the viewer's attention. In *Jaws*, a close-up of the tranquilizer and syringe with which Hooper (Richard Dreyfuss) desperately hopes to neutralize the shark draws the audience's attention to the dramatic significance of the prop (**2.16**).

2.16
A close-up emphasizes the object in *Jaws* (1975).

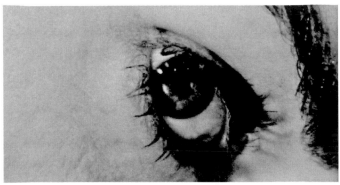

2.17
Scottie (James Stewart) has an epiphany in *Vertigo* (1958).

2.18
An extreme close-up of Marion Crane's lifeless eye in Alfred Hitchcock's *Psycho* (1960).

Close-ups of the human face instill in the viewer a sense of intimacy and identification with the subject; they also increase the level of emotional intensity by magnifying even the subtlest facial expressions. In *Vertigo*, by furrowing his brow and directing his gaze off into the distance, James Stewart signals his character's dawning realization that he has been the victim of an elaborate con game (**2.17**).

The **extreme close-up** is a variation of the close-up shot. It shows only part of the human face—the eyes, for example. In *Psycho* (1960), the themes of scrutiny, guilt, and identity are implied through an extreme close-up of the dead Marion Crane's eye (**2.18**).

Lenses and Depth of Field

Depth of field is the portion of the frame that is in focus in a shot. A small or **shallow depth of field** indicates that only a limited area of the image is in sharp focus, while the rest is blurred. With a large depth of field, or **deep focus**, a large area of the image is in sharp focus.

Wide-angle lenses, which have short focal lengths (12.5–35 mm), have a large depth of field. They exaggerate the sense of depth and distance in a shot while at the same time keeping everything in the frame in focus; they also distort perspective, causing straight lines to appear to curve. Medium or "normal" focal length lenses (35–55 mm) produce shots that correspond to the human eye in terms of perspective and focus. Long or telephoto lenses (75 mm and up) have a shallow depth of field; they flatten the space and make objects appear closer to each other than they actually are. The two photographs below illustrate the different optical effects created by lenses of different focal lengths. **2.19** was photographed with a short lens and thus has a large depth of field. Note how far away the chair appears to be from the statue and also how the furniture in the distance remains in focus. In **2.20**, the longer lens blurs the background while at the same time pulling the chair closer to the statue so that that there appears to be very little depth to the space.

Shallow depth of field can be used to direct the viewer's attention within the frame by focusing on a single figure or object and blurring everything in the foreground and background. The cinematographer also has the ability to redirect

2.19
A lens with a short focal length creates large depth of field.

2.20
A long lens reduces distances, flattens space, and creates a shallow depth of field.

the viewer's attention by shifting focus within the frame. This is known as **racking focus**. In Park Chan-Wook's *Oldboy* (2003), a rack focus is employed as Oh Dae-Su regains consciousness and looks from the bell to the hypnotist's face. Note how the bell and the hypnotist's hand are in focus in **2.21**, while her face is blurred. In **2.22**, the camera shifts focus to the hypnotist's face, blurring her hand and the bell.

During its classical period, Hollywood preferred a photographic style that employed a shallow depth of field. In combination with diffused lighting, this produced what is sometimes described as **"soft focus" cinematography**, which blunted sharp edges and created slightly blurred backgrounds (**2.22**).

While deep focus techniques were in use in the late 1930s, the style didn't achieve its full expression until director Orson Welles and cinematographer Gregg

2.21
Racking focus . . .

2.22
. . . in *Oldboy* (2003).

2.23
Soft focus in Frank Capra's *It Happened One Night* (1934).

Toland used it to such striking effect in *Citizen Kane* in 1941. Deep focus photography allowed cinematographers to shoot longer takes. Because everything in the frame remains in focus, it is not necessary to cut away to a new shot in order to redirect the viewer's attention. Camera movement often takes the places of editing in deep focus photography. In *Citizen Kane*, Welles built sets that could come apart so that the camera could move through walls and furniture (the table in **2.29** actually opened in the center and then closed back up again after the camera dollied through it). In one famous sequence shot, we see a young Charles Foster Kane playing outside in the snow (**2.24**). The camera dollies back to reveal first Mary Kane standing beside the window, looking out at her son (**2.25**), then Walter Thatcher

2.24
A deep-focus sequence shot from *Citizen Kane* (1941).

2.25
Deep focus allows the shot to go from exterior to interior, while keeping figures in both foreground and background in focus.

2.26

2.27

2.28

2.29

The table at which Walter Thatcher and Mary Kane are sitting
was designed to come apart as the camera dollied through it.

looking on (2.26), and finally Jim Kane (2.27). The three adults turn and walk away
from the window as the camera continues to pull back, actually moving through
the table (2.28 and 2.29). In 2.29, Mary Kane and Thatcher sit at the table going
over contracts in the foreground, while Jim Kane stands in the mid-ground protest-
ing and young Charles continues to play outside the window in the background. All
the while, the entire frame remains in focus.

Camera Angles

Camera angle is another element that affects the framing of the shot. While the
specific angle options available to the cinematographer are limitless, they can be
divided into five main types.

The **eye-level shot**, also known as the straight-on shot, is the most commonly
used. The camera is placed about five or six feet off the ground so that it is level with
the subject's face. The eye-level shot does not draw attention to itself and doesn't create

2.30
A low-angle shot in *The Graduate* (1967).

any drama on its own. The viewer tends to experience it as neutral. Whatever dramatic intensity exists in the shot is generated by the action or the subject's expression, not by the camera angle.

The **low-angle shot** increases the perceived height of the subject. In an extreme low-angle shot, the subject will appear to loom over the viewer in a threatening or menacing manner, making this a particularly effective shot to use in thrillers or horror films when photographing assailants and monsters. This shot can also be used to indicate a subject's power or superiority. A low angle shot will increase the apparent speed of moving objects.

The **high-angle shot** or down shot is one in which the camera is placed up high and shoots downward. Objects photographed from this angle appear to be moving more slowly. The high-angle shot tends to diminish the stature of the subject and create an impression of superiority on the part of the viewer. When used in a short/reverse-shot combination (particularly with an alternating low-angle shot), it can imply one character's dominance over another. In *The Graduate* (1967), the low-angle shot of Mr. Braddock emphasizes his patriarchal power and authority, as does the vertical position of his body (**2.30**). The sun shining over his shoulder obscures his face and makes it difficult to look at him without being blinded. The reverse shot of his son Benjamin has the opposite effect. The high camera angle, in combination with Benjamin's horizontal position, serves to diminish his stature (**2.31**). Mr. Braddock looks down on his son both literally and

2.31
A high-angle shot in *The Graduate*.

2.32
An aerial shot tracks the Torrance's car in Stanley Kubrick's *The Shining* (1980).

metaphorically. The shot presents Benjamin as lazy, drifting, lacking ambition, and, all in all, *beneath* his father's expectations.

In the **bird's-eye shot** or aerial shot, the camera is positioned high overhead—on a crane or helicopter, or atop a building or promontory. The point of view created suggests a godlike omniscience in some cases, but it can also be predatory, suggesting something being hunted from the air. Stanley Kubrick's bird's-eye shot of the Torrances' station wagon traveling to the Overlook Hotel in *The Shining* (1980) creates an ominous sense of impending doom as if some evil presence is stalking them from above (**2.32**). Because they are high-angle shots, aerial shots have the effect of slowing down motion. They also drastically reduce the subject's stature and imply vulnerability or insignificance. The bird's-eye shot can be useful in depicting fatigue, death, and, in some cases, transcendence. In *Kill Bill: Vol. 2* an aerial shot of The Bride (Uma Thurman) after she has emerged from being buried alive emphasizes both her exhaustion and the near-death nature of her experience (**2.33**).

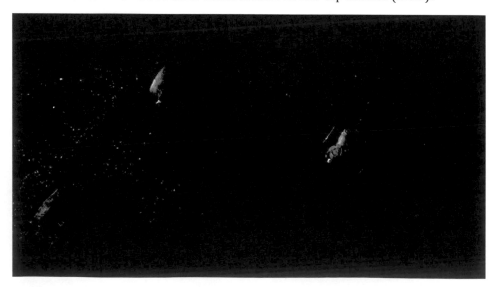

2.33
An aerial shot of The Bride (Uma Thurman) in *Kill Bill: Vol. 2* (2004).

2.34
An oblique-angle shot in Wong Kar-Wai's *Chungking Express* (1994).

The **oblique-angle** or **Dutch-angle shot** is one in which the camera is tilted to one side so that the horizon line is no longer horizontal, but skewed. This shot tends to create a sense of disorientation, chaos, confusion, or tumult, making it effective in portraying everything from a character's state of drunkenness to the effects of an earthquake. In Wong Kar-Wai's *Chungking Express* (1994), the camera is tilted to convey the dizzying sense of sexual excitement experienced by the characters (**2.34**). Note how the horizon line runs diagonally, rather than parallel to the top and bottom of the frame. The shot constitutes a sort of visual pun: the characters are falling for each other romantically, and at the same time they seem to be literally falling to the right side of the frame.

Again, it is important to remember that our observations about various types of shots represent merely general tendencies. An oblique angle shot, for example, does not always indicate disorientation or chaos; it might also be used to create a heightened sense of energy—for instance, in a shot of a speeding train or a herd of galloping horses. When assessing the meaning of a particular shot, always consider its context.

Camera Movements

Unlike still photography, cinema has the ability to employ **mobile framing**. By moving the camera during filming, the cinematographer can move the frame. On a practical level, mobile framing makes it possible to follow the action in a scene by tracking the actors as they move through space. But mobile framing is also an invaluable expressive tool: a specific camera movement can convey a particular set of emotions or induce specific responses in viewers.

In a **pan shot**, the camera does not actually change location, but rather pivots from side to side on a vertical axis created by a tripod or some other piece of mounting equipment. In a pan, the frame will appear to move from left to right or right to left, depending upon the direction of the pan. A pan right, for example, will cause the frame to move from left to right.

In a **tilt shot**, the camera pivots up or down on a horizontal axis. As with a pan, the location of the camera itself does not change. In **2.38** and **2.39**, the dolly move-

2.35
In a single uninterrupted shot from *Taxi Driver* (1976) . . .

2.37
. . . by a dramatic tilt up.

2.38

2.39

2.36
. . . a dolly right is immediately followed . . .

ment has stopped; the camera holds its position and simply tilts upward to reveal Robert De Niro's face.

A **dolly shot** or **tracking shot** is one in which the entire camera moves. (Note how the camera changes position in relation to the fence from **2.36** to **2.37**. In **2.36**, the camera is tilted to the left of the fence; in **2.37**, it has moved to the right of the fence.) Typically, the camera is mounted on a wheeled platform and guided along rails. The camera may move forward and backward, from side to side, or in an arc. As with camera angles, it is impossible to assign a meaning to a particular camera movement without taking into consideration its overall context. A "dolly in" (forward) often creates dramatic intensity and conveys a sense of attraction or heightened interest by giving the impression that the viewer is being drawn toward the subject, but in another situation it may be used as a point-of-view shot to indicate a character's desire to escape from a pursuer.

In a **crane shot** the camera is attached to a movable arm mounted on a motorized vehicle. It allows the camera to move in any direction while floating above the ground, giving the filmmaker the ability to execute complex and often very graceful shots in which the camera swoops and rises. Welles opened *Touch of Evil* (1958) with a three-and-a-half-minute-long crane shot in which the camera swoops and glides above the streets of a Mexican border town.

A **handheld shot** is achieved without use of a tripod or any other type of stabilizing equipment. The result is a jittery frame that is often used by filmmakers to create a heightened sense of realism. Some handheld shots have a documentary feel to them, while others are intended to mimic amateur footage. In *Amores Perros*, Alejandro González Iñárritu uses handheld shots during a hair-raising car chase sequence in order to place the viewer in the middle of the action and capture the panic, fear, and confusion of the characters. In *Eternal Sunshine of the Spotless Mind* (2004), the handheld camera creates a sense of surreptitious intimacy, as if the audience is spying on the private lives of real people.

The **Steadicam**, developed by Garrett Brown in 1976, allows for greater portability and ease of camera movement than does a dolly or a crane. The unit consists of a vest with an articulated arm attached to it. The arm, in turn, attaches to a boom like structure with the camera affixed to the top and a counterbalancing weight at the bottom. The position of the camera and the weight can be reversed into what is called "low mode" in order to place the camera closer to the ground. The Steadicam enables an operator to produce fluid mobile shots without the shaking that usually accompanies handheld shots.

While technically not a camera movement, a **zoom** shot can sometimes resemble a dolly shot. A zoom requires a special lens capable of changing focal lengths. By increasing the focal length (zooming in), the camera operator can enlarge part of the image. As we mentioned in our discussion of depth of field, this enlargement will flatten the image and make objects in the foreground and

2.40
A dolly zoom shot in *Jaws* (1975).

2.41
The track in draws the figures closer . . .

2.42
. . . while the zoom out causes the background to recede.

2.43

background appear to be closer to each other. A dolly movement may be used in combination with a zoom in order to create a visually disturbing effect. The **dolly zoom shot** is achieved by dollying back while simultaneously zooming in on the subject or by dollying in and zooming out simultaneously. The effect was most famously used by Alfred Hitchcock in *Vertigo* to simulate the effect of Scottie's acrophobia. Steven Spielberg also used the shot to capture the reaction of Martin Brody (Roy Scheider) to a shark attack in *Jaws* (**2.40**, **2.41**, **2.42** and **2.43**). As the camera tracks in on Roy Scheider it simultaneously zooms out, creating the unsettling impression that we are moving forward as the background recedes.

Mise-en-Scène

The French term *mise en scène* (pronounced "meez on sen") translates literally as "to put into the scene." The term originated in the theater, where it referred to the placing and arrangement of figures and objects on the stage. The actor up on the proscenium (stage) was part of the mise-en-scène, as was the chair he sat in, the clothes he wore, and the light that perhaps illuminated half his face while casting the other half in shadow.

You get the idea. "Mise-en-scène" (in English, the term typically appears with hyphens and no italics) is an umbrella term encompassing a number of elements such as setting, lighting, props, figure behavior, costume, makeup, and hair. In cinema, it can also be a somewhat confusing term, because different writers use it to refer to different things. Some, such as David Bordwell and Kristin Thompson, define mise-en-scène as only what is placed in front of the camera. Others, such as John Gibbs, challenge this definition, arguing that it is too limited. Gibbs prefers a definition of mise-en-scène that also includes the way in which the staged elements are photographed. "Bordwell and Thompson restrict their definition of mise-en-scene to those elements common to film and theatre. The definition of mise-en-scene therefore makes no reference to framing, camera movement or the position of the camera […] Filmmakers," Gibbs argues, "do not stage the action and only subsequently think about where the camera is going to be placed in order to record it. Similarly to discuss the lighting of a shot without reference to the position of the camera is to misunderstand how films are made. One does not light a set and then set about where the camera is going to be placed. Rather a set is lit with the framing and the movement of the camera absolutely in mind" (54).

Gibbs's point can be illustrated by a shot from *The Graduate* (**3.1**). Our view of Benjamin Braddock's (Dustin Hoffman's) face is partly obstructed by the face of his father, emphasizing the fact that Benjamin has not yet succeeded in forming an identity outside the shadow of his somewhat overbearing parents. In this case, figure position is used effectively to indicate character psychology. But it is a bit disingenuous to say that figure position alone creates this effect. Benjamin's father only appears to obscure his son because of where the camera is located. If the camera were placed in a different

3.1
Both figure position and camera position are necessary to create the impression that Benjamin (Dustin Hoffman) is obscured or obstructed by his father in *The Graduate* (1967).

position (for example, to the right of the frame at 90 degrees to its current position) the result would be entirely different. Benjamin and his father might instead appear to be sitting side by side, both of their faces equally visible in the frame.

Gibbs and those who agree with him define mise-en-scène as the overall *visual* style of the film. Still others, such as the scholar Robin Wood, include editing and sound in their definition of the term—although these are not generally acknowledged as elements of mise-en-scène.

To complicate further the matter of terminology, the term mise-en-scène was also used by the French critic André Bazin to refer to a specific film style that he believed achieved a heightened degree of realism through the use of long takes, depth of field, and spatial unity. Bazin considered mise-en-scène superior to montage style, which emphasized editing.

We can see that mise-en-scène is a contested term, one whose meaning varies depending upon who is using it. This book favors a definition of mise-en-scène that includes cinematography. To define mise-en-scène only as the way in which a scene is staged may be fine for theater, where the viewer's perspective is stationary, but to this author it seems inadequate when discussing cinema, which is an art form that employs a mobile camera and shifting perspectives. Therefore, when the term appears in this book it refers to the visual style of the film, including, as Gibbs puts it, both "the contents of the frame and the way they are organized."

You should be aware of the term's various definitions so that when you encounter it while reading you can determine its intended meaning based upon the context in which it is being used. When writing, you must decide which definition of mise-en-scène you wish to use. Are you using the term to refer to the overall visual style of the film, including camera placement and camera angle (the definition preferred by this book)? Or do you intend the narrower definition of the term: the placement and arrangement of *all the elements that appear in front of the camera*? When writing a paper, one solution to the problem posed by the term is to clarify for the reader which definition you intend. You might want to refer to the specific elements of mise-en-scène that you're discussing; this way you will avoid any possible confusion. For example, if you are writing about Christian symbolism and the theme of redemption in *On the Waterfront*, instead of stating, "The film's mise-en-scène conveys the Christian theme of redemption," you might write, "The film employs setting, costume, props, and figure behavior to express the Christian theme of redemption" or "The film's visual style expresses the Christian theme of redemption."

SETTING

Setting is the place and time in which the events of a film occur. The importance of time to setting should not be overlooked. The New York City of 1995 will look very different from the New York City of 1895.

Even once we have established the time period, the general geographical location of the story tells us something about the setting, but it doesn't provide the entire picture. Let's assume the story occurs in Manhattan in 1995. Is it set in a cramped fifth-floor walk-up on the Lower East Side, or is it set in a spacious Park Avenue townhouse on the Upper East Side . . . or both? Most films make use of several different settings within one or more locales. In *Amores Perros*, for example, the general location is present-day Mexico City, but within the city there are a number of different settings, each of which possesses its own specific atmosphere: there is the bloody dog-fighting arena operated by Mauricio; the cluttered rundown rooms of the house Octavio shares with his mother, his brother, and his sister-in-law (3.2); the squalid hovel in which El Chivo lives, surrounded by the stray dogs he has adopted (3.4), and the bright, orderly apartment of his estranged daughter (3.5); the upper-middle-class home in which Daniel resides with his wife and children (3.6), and the sleek, trendy condo he eventually moves into with Valeria (3.3). Each of these locations reflects a different narrative

3.2
Note the contrast between the drab clutter of Octavio and Susana's space . . .

3.3
. . . and the sterile luxury of Valeria and Daniel's space in *Amores Perros* (2000).

3.4
El Chivo at home . . .

3.5
. . . and in his daughter's apartment.

3.6
Daniel in his daughters' bedroom.

and thematic aspect of the film, and each might be said to represent the psychological and emotional states of the characters who inhabit that particular space. The condo Daniel buys for Valeria represents the carefree life he imagines he will lead with her, unencumbered by the burdens and demands of family life. The bright clean walls and spare lines of the apartment are contrasted with the busy wallpaper pattern and darker décor of the bedroom shared by his daughters. Similarly, the dilapidated disarray of the space El Chivo inhabits reflects the disordered priorities and moral deterioration that have led him to abandon his wife, his daughter, and his academic career and take up the life of a hired assassin. The film's various settings also allow Iñárritu to highlight the differences in socioeconomic status among his characters while at the same time exploring the profound similarities between other aspects of their lives, for example, the romantic longings of Daniel and Octavio or the fraternal rivalries between Octavio and Ramiro and between Gustavo and Luis.

In order to create the desired atmosphere for a particular scene, a filmmaker may either build a set or make use of an existing location. Many films use a combination of the two.

Sets are spaces constructed specifically for the filming of particular scenes. In the early days of film, studios such as Universal constructed open-air sets on their lots in order to take advantage of natural light. Sets for interior rooms were built with three walls (to accommodate the camera) and no ceiling. Typically, a number of such sets would be constructed side by side. Some studios made use of glass walls and ceilings that allowed outside light to enter; shades could be drawn to allow for the use of electric lamps. Later, studios built large windowless facilities that needed to be artificially lit. With the advent of sound, sets were constructed inside large hangar-like soundproof structures referred to as soundstages. A soundstage can house a number of different sets. But soundstage time is exorbitantly expensive, and a resourceful filmmaker may construct indoor sets inside virtually any large enclosed space. For *Eraserhead* (1976), David Lynch built his indoor sets inside an old stable on the grounds of the American Film Institute in Los Angeles, where he was a student. In order to eliminate outside noise, the crew insulated the walls with fiberglass batting covered by tarps. For his 2009 independent production *In the Darkness*, filmmaker Andrew Robinson transformed his home's two-car garage into a soundstage.

Studio sets allow filmmakers a high degree of control over a scene's setting. They can be more precisely lit than locations; unwanted noise can be more easily blocked out; background activity, such as automobile traffic or pedestrian foot traffic, is not a factor; and weather conditions can be simulated to suit the requirements of the scene. It would have been impossible, for example, to shoot most of the live action shots for *The Perfect Storm* (2000) out on the open sea. Instead these scenes were shot on a studio set where wind, rain, and waves were simulated in a large water tank. By closely controlling the environment, director Wolfgang Petersen was able to capture the footage he wanted while minimizing any risk to the actors and crew. Even a far more placid setting can sometimes be better reproduced on a set. Orson Welles shot the snow scene for *Citizen Kane* on a soundstage with fake snow blown in by the crew. Such methods sometimes present their own hazards: production stills from the film reveal crew members wearing respirator masks to filter out the particles.

Not all sets are enclosed. Filmmakers also construct outdoor sets, often on the back lots of studios. This is particularly common in films, such as westerns, in which the architecture must conform to a particular time period. For *The Man Who Shot Liberty Valance* (1962), while John Ford shot some exteriors for the town of Shinbone indoors on Paramount's soundstages (3.7), he filmed others outside on MGM's Lot 3 (3.8; arrows indicate a painted backdrop and false facades).

Unlike sets, **locations** are actual places chosen by filmmakers (or their location scouts) because they suit the requirements of the story and enhance its believability. Milos Forman shot *One Flew over the Cuckoo's Nest* on location in an actual mental institution and cast the institution's doctors and patients in some roles, lending the film a sense of authenticity that it might have otherwise lacked. Similarly, Martin Scorsese filmed *Taxi Driver* on the streets of New York City during the sweltering summer of 1975 with racial tensions rising and the city teetering on the brink of bankruptcy. "That summer was a down point for New York," Scorsese later recalled, "and it shows in that film, in the mood of it. It was so hot you could see the violence shimmering in the air, taste it in your mouth, and there we were in the middle of it" (quoted in Keyser 68). The New York City that appears on screen is a nightmarish inferno, a Dantesque underworld that reflects the tormented psyche of the film's protagonist, Travis Bickle.

Conversely, a director's decision to shoot a particular scene on set rather than on location can compromise a film's visual aesthetics. This is certainly the case with some of Ford's films, including *The Man Who Shot Liberty Valance*, in which the exterior scenes shot on a soundstage have the feel of a 1960s television production. Ford's assistant director Wingate Smith complained that

3.7
An exterior set constructed on a Paramount soundstage for *The Man Who Shot Liberty Valance* (1962).

3.8
The arrival of the train in *Liberty Valance* was shot on an MGM back lot.

3.9
In *Citizen Kane* (1941) . . .

3.10
. . . a wipe creates the illusion . . .

3.11
. . . of a vast space.

the set didn't look "lived in." Even *The Searchers*, most of which Ford shot on location in Monument Valley, Utah, contains some studio scenes that are robbed of their naturalism by the stagy look of the Hollywood sets on which they were filmed.

Sometimes sets are constructed on location. The set for the city of Edoras in *The Lord of the Rings: The Two Towers* (2002) was built amid mountains in a glacial valley in New Zealand. The construction department had to first erect a steel frame for the set and then drill into the side of a cliff in order to anchor it amid the valley's high winds. They then covered the steel frame with wood. In order to minimize environmental impact, the area's natural vegetation had to be removed prior to set construction, temporarily transplanted, and then moved back after shooting.

Settings can also be created with special effects. *Citizen Kane* employs shots that combine studio-built sets with miniatures and painted mattes. The transition from the plaster miniature used to create Walther Thatcher's statue (3.9) to the live-action shot of the reporter Thompson arriving at the Thatcher Library (3.11) is accomplished by means of a **wipe**—a transition in which an optical line moves across the frame, in this case from top to bottom, replacing the old image with a new one. Here the line is almost invisible, creating a nearly seamless transition between the shot of the miniature and the live action shot (you can make out the disguised edge of the wipe on the right side of the pedestal in **3.10** where the tones don't quite match). The effect allowed Welles to create at little cost the illusion of an austerely grandiose space, suggesting that Thatcher's ego, while more puritanical, may have been no less monumental than Kane's own. Kane's campaign speech scene (3.12) also achieves the appearance of a vast space by means of special effects cinematography. The shot is actually a composite of three different live-action shots—the stage (A), the two small figures to the right of the stage (B), and the balcony from which Boss Geddes looks on (C)—and a painted matte of the audience (D). Tiny holes were punched in the matte and lights shone from behind in order to create the illusion of movement.

The special effects cinematography used in *Citizen Kane* and many other films to create fades, dissolves, wipes, superimpositions, and composites employed an optical printer, a device which makes it possible to copy film by re-photographing it. In **3.12**, the various

3.12
Three separate live-action shots (A, B, and C) were combined with a painted matte shot (D) to create the setting for this one shot from *Citizen Kane*.

components of the composite (A, B, C, and D) were rephotographed as a single image using an optical printer. With the advent of computer-generated imagery (CGI), settings that previously were created with mattes and an optical printer are now achieved digitally.

ACTING

Film differs from literature in a number of ways, but none more crucial than the fact that films do not have access to a character's interior life in the same way that works of literature do. In a literary work, an omniscient third-person narrator may report the thoughts of multiple characters without it seeming disruptive or intrusive. In the following excerpt from Peter Benchley's novel *Jaws*, for example, the omniscient narrator moves freely between the thoughts of Martin Brody and those of his wife, Ellen:

> Ellen Brody was thirty-six, five years younger than her husband, and the fact that she looked barely thirty was a source of both pride and annoyance to Brody: pride because, since she looked handsome and young and was married to him, she made him seem a man of excellent taste and substantial attraction; annoyance because she had been able to keep her good looks despite the strains of bearing three children, whereas Brody—though hardly fat at six-foot-one and two hundred pounds—was beginning to be concerned about his blood pressure and his thickening middle. Sometimes during the summer, Brody would catch himself gazing with idle lust at one of the young, long-legged girls who pranced

around town—their untethered breasts bouncing beneath the thinnest of cotton jerseys. But he never enjoyed the sensation, for it always made him wonder whether Ellen felt the same stirring when she looked at the tanned, slim young men who so perfectly complemented the long-legged girls. And as soon as that thought occurred to him, he felt still worse, for he recognized it as a sign that he was on the unfortunate side of forty and had already lived more than half his life.

 Summers were bad times for Ellen Brody, for in summer she was tortured by thoughts she didn't want to think—thoughts of chances missed and lives that could have been. She saw people she had grown up with: prep school classmates now married to bankers and brokers, summering in Amity and wintering in New York, graceful women who stroked tennis balls and enlivened conversations with equal ease, women who (Ellen was convinced) joked among themselves about Ellen Shepherd marrying that policeman because he got her pregnant in the back seat of his 1948 Ford, which had not been the case (Benchley 13-4).

After revealing Martin's thoughts about his wife in the first paragraph, Benchley makes us privy to Ellen's thoughts about her marriage to Martin. In order to give an audience similar access to a character's thoughts and feelings, a filmmaker would have to use a voiceover. In this case, the filmmaker would need two separate voiceovers, one for Martin and one for Ellen. Even in self-consciously artistic films the use of multiple voiceovers is rare (Terence Malik's *Days of Heaven* (1978) and Wim Wenders's *Wings of Desire* (1987) are two exceptions)—and for good reason. The technique is cumbersome. Even the more conventional single voiceover runs the risk of distracting viewers and diminishing the power of a film by explaining what might otherwise be dramatically illustrated through action and dialogue. In the case of *Jaws*, the use of multiple voiceovers in the film would have certainly been more of a distraction than a valuable addition to the story. When Steven Spielberg adapted Benchley's novel for the screen, he did so without employing any voiceover whatsoever. Instead, he relied on the words and actions of his actors to convey the interior lives of the characters.

 Film is primarily a visual medium, and filmmakers have long abided by the imperative "Show; don't tell." Through their physical appearance, their gestures, and even their position in the frame, actors can "show" the audience the thoughts and feelings of the characters on the screen. The value that cinema has historically placed on appearances is underscored by the fact that so many of its biggest stars conform to conventional standards of beauty. Thus Denzel Washington, George Clooney, Halle Berry, and Julia Roberts are more likely to be cast in leading roles than are Danny DeVito, Steve Buscemi, and Kathy Bates. It also means that certain types of roles are often associated with certain physical attributes. Protagonists usually conform to conventional standards of beauty, while antagonists often possess physical attributes that distance viewers from them in some way—outright disfigurements, as in the case of Darth Vader, or simply unusual features, as in the case of *Fargo*'s Carl Showalter, played by Steve Buscemi (**3.13**). With his slight build, stooped posture, sallow complexion, bulging eyes, crooked teeth, weak chin, and receding hairline, Buscemi doesn't fit the traditional Hollywood definition of "handsome." As a result, he is often cast as a villain. In a *New Yorker* profile piece, Buscemi told John Lahr that "Tarantino hired him [for *Reservoir Dogs* (1992)] because he thought he looked like a criminal" (Lahr). And yet, Buscemi's appearance and demeanor also convey a frailty and vulnerability that don't quite fit the description of the standard Hollywood bad guy. As Lahr points out, "Buscemi is almost never just a cold-blooded killer; he is also a hilarious victim." This is almost certainly part of what attracted Tarantino to him for the role of the manic Mr. Pink.

3.13
Steve Buscemi as Carl Showalter in Joel and Ethan Coen's *Fargo* (1996).

Buscemi's *Reservoir Dogs* anecdote illustrates the degree to which filmmakers rely on **casting** (the selection of actors for roles) to convey meaning in a film. How important is casting? Imagine Danny DeVito in the role of the Terminator instead of Arnold Schwarzenegger. DeVito is a talented actor, but he doesn't possess the physical attributes to convincingly play the role of a cyborg assassin. Casting DeVito in the role would have turned James Cameron's film into a sci-fi parody rather than an apocalyptic allegory.

In mainstream cinema, acting often places an emphasis on realism or naturalism—on the extent to which it resembles a generally agreed upon conception of reality. Critics and audiences judge actors based upon the degree to which their portrayals reflect convincing behaviors, recognizable emotions, and responses that seem appropriate to given situations. Meryl Streep, who is chameleonlike in her ability to slip into personas, adopt mannerisms, and mimic accents, is thus hailed by many as the greatest actor of her generation. What audiences admire about Streep is that the emotions, gestures, and responses of her characters are recognizable and familiar—they resemble the behavior of real people.

But "real" is a tricky term. Can we say with any certainty what constitutes real or convincing behavior in a given situation? The notion of "reality" espoused by conventional cinema is not a matter of objective fact, but is rather a construct—an invention, determined to a large degree by social, economic, and political factors. To a great degree, audiences have been conditioned to expect specific behaviors from particular types of characters in particular situations. If an actor exhibits the behavior we expect, we tend to praise her acting as "realistic" or "believable." Acting that falls outside the range of convention is often characterized by mainstream viewers as "not believable" or "bad."

Let's imagine we are filming a scene for a movie set in Germany during the years immediately following World War II. Our protagonist is a young German woman whose husband has not returned home from the war. She has finally given up hope that he is alive. Economic conditions are terrible. The country is in ruins. In order to survive, our protagonist works at a bar for black American GIs. She meets an American soldier there and develops a relationship with him. She likes him a great deal, but reserves her love for the husband she has lost. The GI is kind to her and generous to her family. One afternoon they are making love in her room when her long-lost husband appears at the door. How would the protagonist react? What would be realistic behavior on her part? She would certainly react with surprise at the sight of the husband whom she'd thought dead. She might faint from shock or cry out with joy at the realization that the man she loves is still alive . . . she might also react with embarrassment and shame at the fact that he has found her in bed with a lover. And the husband? He might storm off in anger or tear her from the arms of her lover and then break down in tears at the circumstances that have kept him from her and led her to rely on another man for her survival.

In fact, this is a scene from an actual film, Rainer Werner Fassbinder's *The Marriage of Maria Braun* (1979). In Fassbinder's film, however, the actors portray behaviors quite different from those described above. When Maria (Hanna Schygulla) notices her husband Hermann (Klaus Lowitsch) standing in the doorway (**3.14** and **3.15**), she doesn't gasp or shout out in surprise. Nor does she express the slightest hint of shame. Instead she smiles and says in a calm, slightly dreamy voice to her lover, Bill (George Byrd), "Look, Bill. It's Hermann" (**3.16**). She rushes to Hermann, who slaps her (**3.17**). She falls. Bill gets up from the bed and goes to her side (**3.18**). Hermann meanwhile neither shouts angrily nor cries, but peers cautiously into the room, spots a pack of cigarettes on a table, rushes over, and greedily lights one up (**3.19–3.21**). He sits on the bed calmly smoking (**3.23**) and then begins clawing at the bed sheets. Bill restrains him. Hermann goes limp. Bill appears to tenderly embrace him as Maria walks up behind Bill and smashes a bottle over Bill's head, killing

3.14
In *The Marriage or Maria Braun* (1979) . . .

3.15
Hermann returns . . .

3.16
. . . to find Maria with a lover.

3.17

3.18

3.19

3.20

3.21

him. Maria looks at Hermann and smiles. She appears to feel no horror or remorse over killing Bill. No one asks any questions or offers any explanations or apologies. Other than Maria's matter-of-fact statement "It's Hermann," none of the characters says anything at all during the scene.

At first glance, the acting seems unnatural, the behavior of the characters dissociated from the actual situation they find themselves in. None of the actors appears to express the appropriate emotions. A viewer accustomed to watching more conventional films might complain that the acting is unrealistic—that after returning from a Russian POW camp after years of war and finding his wife in bed with another man, Hermann would not sit silently on the bed smoking; that after smashing a bottle over Bill's head, Maria would not smile obliviously at Hermann. But in many ways, this "unrealistic" portrayal of the scene is more

3.22

3.23

real than any conventional interpretation would have been, as Hanna Schygulla explained in an interview:

> There's this unusual scene that you can't really get over where she's with her black lover, whom she really likes and with whom she feels comfortable, but whom she never really loves because she's saved up her love for someone else. And while she's busy with him, Hermann has finally returned and stands in the doorway. When she sees him there, she doesn't have a guilty conscience, but beams with happiness. I couldn't have imagined a reaction like this. [Fassbinder] told me that he wanted it this way. She must not be caught up in any feelings of guilty conscience. She's above that. That made it trancelike, almost unreal just like some atrocities or some of the shocking moments in life are. But that is exactly what he wanted. He wanted something that goes beyond morals. He wanted to push forward into another space where those things are not valid.

In addition to shedding light on the motivation behind her performance, Schygulla's account indicates the degree to which an actor's choices are sometimes determined by a director. In this case, Fassbinder's direction resulted in performances that play down the reactions of the characters to a degree that may seem unnatural to some viewers.

At the opposite end of the spectrum, an excessively demonstrative performance may also be characterized as unnatural. In *Lola* (1981), Fassbinder encouraged "exaggerated acting by the cast to the point of caricature" (Toteberg 31). According to actor Armin Mueller-Stahl, "We played at the most excessive level, actually often beyond that, entering the red zone" (quoted in Toteberg 31). Actors who give such performances are often accused of "chewing up the scenery" or overacting. In a review of Stanley Kubrick's *The Shining*, *Variety* criticized both Jack Nicholson (3.24) and Shelley Duvall (3.25) for giving over-the-top performances: "The crazier Nicholson gets, the more idiotic he looks. Shelley Duvall transforms the warm sympathetic wife of the book into a simpering, semi-retarded hysteric."

Unnatural performances can create an emotional distance between the character and the viewer. The German playwright Bertolt Brecht referred to this as the **alienation effect** or the **A-effect**. Brecht believed that when a viewer's emotional response was suppressed through alienation, the viewer was better able to critically engage the larger social issues raised by the work. He was not interested in having his actors create believable illusions or elicit empathy on the part of the audience. "The technique which produces the A-effect is the exact opposite of that which aims at empathy," Brecht wrote. By refusing to "become" the character he is playing, the actor makes it possible for the audience to adopt a more critical attitude toward the events being portrayed: "Because he [the actor] doesn't identify himself with him he can pick a

3.24
Jack Nicholson . . .

3.25
. . . and Shelley Duvall in *The Shining* (1980).

definite attitude to adopt towards the character whom he portrays, can show what he thinks of him and invite the spectator, who is likewise not asked to identify himself, to criticize the character portrayed" (Brecht 139).

One of the difficulties we face when characterizing a performance is that different viewers respond differently to the same performance. While the *Variety* critic was alienated by Nicholson's performance in *The Shining*, *New York Times* critic Janet Maslin found his performance compelling and effective: "Mr. Nicholson's Jack is one of his most vibrant characterizations, furiously alive in every frame and fueled by an explosive anger." In short, Maslin found Nicholson's portrayal to be realistic and convincing, while the *Variety* critic did not.

Another difficulty in judging "realistic" acting is that audiences' expectations evolve over time. In the 1950s, audiences watching Marlon Brando in *A Streetcar Named Desire* (1951) and James Dean in *Rebel without a Cause* (1954) were likely to view those intensely emotional performances as very realistic. But contemporary viewers are more likely to see those performances as highly stylized and exaggerated.

Facial Expression, Figure Position, and Figure Movement

Figure position and figure movement are important elements of mise-en-scène. In cinema, **figure** is a broad term that refers to any object within the frame, including architectural elements, natural elements (such as trees or mountains), furniture, people, and animals. Of all these, the human figure, in the form of the actor, is often the most significant. The facial expressions, positions, and movements of the actors all contribute considerably to the creation of meaning in a film.

Because the camera can capture physical details and nuances that would go unnoticed by a theater audience viewing a performance from a distance, acting for the cinema tends to be more understated than acting for the stage. On film, subtle facial expressions—the direction of an actor's gaze, the slightest furrowing of a brow—can convey a wealth of information. In *Double Indemnity*, Walter Neff's guilty conscience is indicated by the fact that he cannot bring himself to directly face Lola Dietrichson (3.26), the daughter of the man he's murdered. Instead, Neff (Fred MacMurray) glances sideways at her as she speaks (3.27). When Lola tells him that she believes Phyllis killed her mother, his gaze shifts away from her and settles somewhere off in the distance (3.28), making it clear that her words have caused him to suspect Phyllis may have set him up.

3.26
In *Double Indemnity* (1944) . . .

3.27
. . . Fred MacMurray conveys his character's thoughts . . .

3.28
. . . with his eyes.

3.29
Bill (David Carradine) and Kiddo (Uma Thurman) face off against a desolate backdrop in *Kill Bill: Vol. 2* (2004).

Figure position, the arrangement of the figures in the frame, can convey a great deal about character psychology, character relationships, and theme. The proximity of or distance between characters from scene to scene often indicates emotional closeness or distance. In *Kill Bill: Vol. 2*, the desert space visible between The Bride (Uma Thurman) and Bill (David Carradine) (**3.29**) reflects the emotional distance between them and foreshadows the violence that is about to erupt at the wedding rehearsal. Note how the two characters are shown in opposing profiles located at opposite ends of the frame as if they are about to face off against each other.

In *Cat People* (1942), figure position is used to chart the shifting relationships in the romantic triangle between Irena (Simone Simon), Oliver (Kent Smith), and Alice (Jane Randolph), as well as to express themes such as fate and the conflict between the rational and the irrational. At Irena and Oliver's wedding party, Irena is positioned between Oliver and Alice. Irena and Oliver sit with their shoulders touching and their faces turned toward each other, while Alice sits a slight distance apart from them (**3.30**). The positions of the actors emphasize the bond between Oliver and Irena, and the subsequent two-shots clearly separate the married couple from Alice (**3.31** and **3.32**).

3.30
Figure position bonds Oliver and Irena (left) in *Cat People* (1942).

3.31
Framing emphasizes the bond between the couple . . .

3.32
. . . while excluding Alice.

However, as Oliver becomes estranged from Irena and grows closer to Alice, the figure positions change significantly. In the museum scene later in the film, Oliver and Alice stand close to each other—in fact, their figures overlap—while Irena stands apart from them (**3.33**). The model ship emphasizes all that Oliver and Alice have in common (they both work for the same shipbuilding company) while the figurehead of the cat on the ship's prow identifies Irena with the ancient curse that serves as an obstacle to her sexual relationship with Oliver. The ship, which obstructs Oliver and Alice but not Irena, represents the rational modern world and

3.33
Figure position signals a change in relationship dynamics in *Cat People*.

3.34
The characters move . . .

3.35
. . . in opposite directions.

perhaps also indicates their inability to see anything that doesn't conform to their rational worldview—which is why they assume that the curse of the cat people isn't real and that Irena needs psychiatric help. The ship's rigging forms a kind of web that ensnares the three characters and seems to imply that they are all trapped by fate, victims of larger forces that they cannot control. In the next shot (**3.36**), Irena's proximity to the statue of Anubis emphasizes her status as "the Other," foreign, mysterious, and dangerous.

Figure position does not remain static in a film. Figures move, and figure movement is an important element of mise-en-scène. In the museum scene in *Cat People*, Irena is excluded from the conversation by Oliver and Alice, who insist that she must find the ship exhibit boring and encourage her to go off and look at paintings on her own. Irena first protests, then turns her back on Oliver and Alice and begins to walk away (**3.34**). She pauses in the doorway and watches them as they walk off in the opposite direction, enthusiastically discussing a drawing of a ship (**3.35**). Irena's movements (turning and walking away, looking back, watching Oliver and Alice from a distance) imply hurt feelings, resentment, and finally jealousy as she observes her husband absorbed in conversation with another woman, while the movements of Oliver and Alice indicate Oliver's increasing distance from Irena and his growing affection for Alice. The scene underscores the way in which Oliver and Alice patronize and infantilize Irena. She is like a child being sent off so that her parents can discuss adult things. The fact that Oliver and Alice do not glance back at her demonstrates how absorbed they are in each other and how oblivious they are to her feelings.

Figure movement can do more than just reveal character psychology. In *On the Waterfront*, it performs an aesthetic function while at the same time underscoring the film's themes. When Terry releases the pigeon, the bird's movement draws our eye up to the rooftop where Johnny Friendly's goons wait for Joey Doyle. The pigeon's upward flight, which perhaps represents Terry's desire for freedom and transcendence, is counterbalanced by the downward plunge of Joey's body. The two movements imply that flight is impossible, that there is no escape from the violence of the streets below. Joey is, after all, associated with a bird—he is referred to as both a pigeon and a canary. "Maybe he could sing," Truck jokes, "but he couldn't fly." Joey's fall from the rooftop sets the tone for the opening of the film and ties into its Christian theme by hinting at the fallen state of man and the unlikely prospect of transcendence on the waterfront.

3.36
Figure position aligns Irena with dark, mysterious forces represented by the statue of the Egyptian god of the dead, Anubis.

Costume, Makeup, and Hair

Costumes (the clothing worn by the characters) may function on several different levels in a film. They may help to establish setting and circumstances, reveal character psychology, move the plot forward, or convey theme.

As we mentioned above, exposition refers to the setup of a story. It poses a number of challenges for a filmmaker. The circumstances of a given environment and the backstories of relevant characters must be established quickly and efficiently in a film. With a few rare exceptions, there is no authorial voice or omniscient third-person narrator to fill us in on the backstories of the characters or the circumstances in which they find themselves when the story opens. Dialogue must be used sparingly to convey exposition. It will appear unnatural for characters to stand around describing their backgrounds and motivations. It is also not very exciting to watch. If filmmakers want to avoid boring their audiences, they must find other, less intrusive, means of communicating the information necessary to the setup of the story. Costume can play an important role here.

A character's style of dress can help establish the setting of a film by indicating a particular place and time period. In Kenji Mizoguchi's *Ugetsu* (1953) (**3.37**), the traditional kimonos and samurai armor are indicative of sixteenth-century Japan, while in Yasujiro Ozu's *An Autumn Afternoon* (1962) (**3.38**), the gray flannel business suits signal that the action unfolds in the modern Japan of the early 1960s.

Costume can be used not only to recreate a familiar present or a vanished past, but to conjure up an imaginary future. Fritz Lang's *Metropolis* (1927), set in 2026,

3.37
Kenji Mizoguchi's *Ugetsu* (1953).

3.38
Yasujiro Ozu's *An Autumn Afternoon* (1962).

imagines a dystopian future in which a bitter scientist, Rotwang, seeks revenge against his rival, the wealthy capitalist Fredersen, by creating a mechanical woman who deceives the city's workers and incites them to rebellion (**3.39**). Brigitte Helm, who played the robot, wore a costume fabricated out of a wood filler compound that was molded to her body and painted to resemble metal. Costume can also serve as a means by which a filmmaker alludes to another film. The metal bands that encircle Maria (also played by Helm) in the creation scene (**3.40**), for example, are alluded to in the costume worn by Leeloo after she is reconstituted in *The Fifth Element* (1997) (**3.41**), Luc Besson's sci-fi tale set in the twenty-third century. For that film, fashion

3.39
Brigitte Helm wears a robot costume fabricated out of wood filler compound in Fritz Lang's *Metropolis* (1927)

3.40
The creation scene in Metropolis . . .

3.41
. . . is alluded to by the costume Jean-Paul Gauthier designed for
Leeloo in *The Fifth Element* (1997).

designer Jean-Paul Gauthier created over 950 mostly futuristic outfits to clothe an
array of human and nonhuman characters (**3.42** and **3.43**).

In addition to helping establish setting, clothing can tell us a great deal about a
character, such as his social status, his character traits, or his perception of himself.
The beat-up bowler hat, torn gloves, and threadbare suit worn by Charlie Chaplin's
tramp in *City Lights* (1931) (**3.44**) reveal his destitution and indicate his determi-
nation to maintain his dignity in the face of poverty. The outfit also distinguishes
him from the well-dressed and hypocritical civic leaders who prattle on about
"peace and prosperity" while they chase away an individual in dire need of both. A

3.42
Gauthier's costumes . . .

3.43
. . . in *The Fifth Element*.

3.44
Chaplin's tramp in *City Lights* (1931).

3.45
Marion Crane's dual nature . . .

3.46
. . . expressed through lingerie in *Psycho* (1960).

character is usually associated with a particular style of dress, and a change in costume may accompany a change in the character, as is the case with the tramp when the rich man befriends him and takes him out to a nightclub. Drunk and dressed in tails, the unassuming tramp transforms into a crude, aggressive lout. In *Psycho*, Marion Crane's (Janet Leigh's) change from white (**3.45**) to black lingerie (**3.46**) signals a shift in her character (she's decided to steal $40,000 from her employer) and reveals her dual nature.

Jeff Bailey (Robert Mitchum), the protagonist of Jacques Tourneur's film noir *Out of the Past*, appears early in the film amid bucolic surroundings dressed in casual sportsman's attire (**3.47**). Later, when he reveals his real name—Jeff Markham—and his sordid past to Ann, he appears in the prototypical noir detective's outfit that he wore in his previous life: a trench coat and a fedora (**3.48**). The change in costume suggests that the inescapable pull of his past has already begun to transform him back into the man he was, drawing him away from Ann and sealing his doom.

A costume element can also serve as the hinge upon which a key plot point turns. In *Vertigo*, after recognizing Judy's necklace as the same one worn by Carlotta Valdes in her portrait, Scottie realizes that Judy and Madeline are the same person and that he has been the victim of an elaborate con. In *Ugetsu*, Tobei's pursuit of a spear and armor leads him to abandon his wife, Ohama, who is raped by soldiers and must resort to prostitution in order to survive.

3.47
In *Out of the Past* (1947), Jeff Bailey (Robert Mitchum) . . .

3.48
. . . is pulled back into his shady past.

This example from *Ugetsu* also illustrates the way in which costumes can elucidate theme and help to reveal a film's underlying meaning. In Miyazaki's film, the samurai spear and armor are a costume in a double sense: first, the armor serves as a costume for the actor playing the role of Tobei (Eitaro Ozawa); second, it functions within the film as a costume for the peasant Tobei, allowing him to impersonate a samurai. For Tobei, the armor symbolizes power, status, and glory. The fact that Tobei becomes a samurai without having done anything to earn the title (he did not kill the general whose head he delivers to the victorious commander) suggests that military glory is ultimately an illusion, that the heroism of warriors is often based on myths. In fact, the com-

3.49
Red (Ron Perlman) files his horns in *Hellboy* (2004).

mander does not believe Tobei's claim but rewards him anyway, underscoring the hypocrisy of the military elite. The price Tobei pays for his glory—the suffering, misery, and degradation of his wife—is too high.

Costume is used in a similar way, but to the opposite effect, in *On the Waterfront*, where Joey Doyle's jacket becomes a symbol of courage and self-sacrifice. Following Joey's murder, Pop Doyle gives the jacket to "Kayo" Dugan. Dugan, who eventually testifies against the mob, is wearing Joey's jacket in the hatch when he is killed by Johnny Friendly's crew in a deliberate act made to look like an accident. Edie Doyle then gives the jacket to Terry, who wears it during his climactic confrontation with Friendly. The jacket represents Terry's transformation into a hero—like Joey, he is willing to sacrifice himself in order to redeem his fellow longshoremen.

Like costume, makeup and hairstyle are means of "dressing" the human figure and can be used to establish time and place, reveal a character's psychology and circumstances, signal a change in a character, or elucidate theme. In *Hellboy* (2004), Red's filed-down horns (**3.49**) reveal his ambivalence about his demonic origins and his desire to assimilate into human society, while Harvey Dent's makeup and hair in *The Dark Knight* (**3.50**) serve as a visual representation of the film's key themes: duality and corruption.

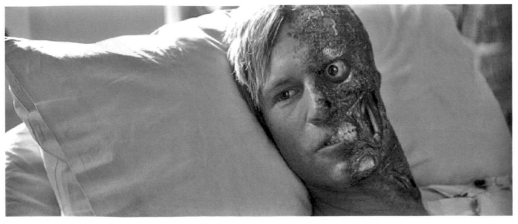

3.50
Duality and corruption: Harvey Dent (Aaron Eckhart) in *The Dark Knight* (2008).

3.51
Loretta Castorini (Cher) . . .

3.52
. . . is transformed by love in *Moonstruck* (1987).

Sometimes the goal is to conceal flaws and accentuate desirable features in order to make the actor appear glamorous; other times, the goal is to de-glamorize the actor. In *Vertigo*, Judy's overdone make-up gives her the appearance of a crude copy of the more sophisticated Madeleine, while her hairdo with its mousy brown curlicues looks fussed-over and tawdry in contrast to Madeleine's elegant platinum blond bun, indicating the gap between the real Judy and the role that she must play in order to appease Scottie's male fantasy. In *Moonstruck* (1987), the repressed Loretta (Cher) dresses in drab clothes and wears her graying hair in a frumpy bun (**3.51**). When she finally emerges from her shell, her emotional transformation is signaled by a glamorous costume and hairstyle (**3.52**).

Animatronics in *The Fifth Element:* Costume, Makeup, and Robotics Converge

In some films, dressing the actors is quite a complicated affair. Luc Besson's over-the-top 1997 sci-fi flick *The Fifth Element* set a new standard for special effects and production design in the genre. "Besson gives us one great visual conceit after another," Roger Ebert wrote in his review of the film. One of these visual conceits was the alien race of Mangalores (**3.56**). Creating these creatures required the skills of team of artists working under the direction of Creature Effects Supervisor Nick Dudman.

The creature effects field combines the skills of costume design, makeup, and animatronic modeling. Animatronics is a cross between robotics and puppetry. In order to create an animatronic creature such as Jean-Baptiste Emanuel Zorg's pet, Picasso, a mechanized skeleton employing servos and paddles is first constructed in order to give the creature lifelike motion. Then a skin fabricated out of latex or some similar material is placed over this skeleton.

In the case of an animatronic costume such as the one used to create the Mangalores, the process is even more complicated. Batteries, motors, and other mechanical components must be concealed inside the costume, while at the same time the costume must conform to the actor's body. In addition, a method for controlling the mechanical components is required.

Dudman's team began by constructing mechanical skulls for the Mangalores (**3.53**). The skins were then cast from

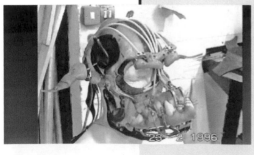

3.53
A mechanical Mangalore skull with animatronic components.

3.54
The skin of a Mangalore mask.

3.55
A puppeteer manipulates a Mangalore's facial expression by means of radio controls.

3.56
The animatronic Mangalore costumes as they appear onscreen in Luc Besson's *The Fifth Element*.

sculptures (3.54) and placed over the skulls. The completed mask with their animatronic components were then fitted over the heads of the actors. Puppeteers stationed offscreen manipulated each Mangalore's facial expressions, including lip, brow, and ear movements, by means of radio transmitters (3.55).

Props

Properties (usually referred to as **props**) are moveable objects that appear in a film. They may form part of a setting's decor, as in the case of the furniture, art objects, or electronic equipment in a room. Or they may be associated with an individual character's costume as in the case of a gun or a wheelchair. As with the other elements of mise-en-scène, props can provide viewers with important information about plot, character, and theme.

In *Rear Window*, Mrs. Thorwald's wedding ring functions as a plot device. Lisa's discovery of the ring confirms Jeff's suspicion that Thorwald has murdered his wife. But the ring also provides information about character psychology and theme. By placing the ring on her finger, Lisa reveals, either consciously or unconsciously, her own wish to marry Jeff. At the same time, the ring's presence on

Lisa's finger symbolically associates her with the murdered Mrs. Thorwald and thus hints at Jeff's desire to get rid of Lisa just as Lars Thorwald has gotten rid of his wife. François Truffaut sees the ring as a symbol of Lisa's victory in her quest to get Jeffries to propose to her, while Tania Modleski points out that "Lisa's ardent desire for marriage leads straight to a symbolic wedding with a wife-murderer [Thorwald];" in her opinion, the ring "may be read as pointing up the victimization of women by men" (Modleski 78).

Whether one agrees with Truffaut or Modleski, the important point here is that a careful examination of the role played by a key prop can serve as an entryway into an interpretation of an entire film.

Lighting

Cinematographers are fond of referring to cinematography as "painting with light." The phrase has been used so often over the years that it has become a cliché, but it indicates just how important light is to the filmmaking process. While lenses, filters, film stock, and processing are all important when it comes to lighting, our discussion will be limited to an explanation of basic lighting techniques and an examination of the ways in which lighting functions as an aspect of the film's mise-en-scène or style.

While the lighting techniques used in contemporary films are often quite sophisticated and complex, **three-point lighting,** developed under the Hollywood studio system during the classical period, remains the basis for lighting design in the industry. As its name suggest, three-point lighting consists of three light sources: a key light, a fill light, and a backlight (3.57).

The **key light** is the brightest light source. It is placed to one side of the camera so that it illuminates the scene from an angle; this angle will vary depending upon the desired effect. For example, a key light placed close to the camera will cast a fairly direct and even light on the actor's face. However, a key light placed farther off to one side will illuminate only part of the actor's face while casting the remainder in shadow.

The **fill light** is used in combination with a key light. Positioned on the side of the subject opposite the key light, it is less intense than the key. Its purpose is to reduce or eliminate the harsh shadows created by the key light.

Backlighting originates from behind and usually above the subject. Used alone or in conjunction with very low key and fill lighting, it creates a silhouette effect. Used with higher levels of key and fill, backlighting will highlight a subject's edges, accentuate the subject's three-dimensional nature, and differentiate the subject from the background.

High-key lighting refers to a setup in which the fill light and backlight are nearly as bright as the key light. Typically, the key to fill light ratio is 2:1 or lower. As a result, shadows are diminished or rendered transparent and the overall effect is of a soft, evenly distributed light (3.58). The mood created by such a design ranges from neutral to upbeat, making it the lighting scheme of choice for comedies, romances, and action–adventure films.

Low-key lighting is achieved by increasing the ratio of key to fill light. In other words, the fill light and backlight are much less intense than the key. This creates high contrast. Some areas of the subject will be brightly lit while other areas are in deep shadow. The resulting effect, known as **chiaroscuro**, is moody and ominous. Low-key lighting

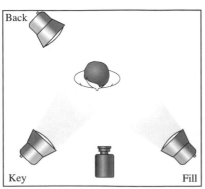

3.57
Three-point lighting.

3.58
High-key lighting in *Legally Blonde* (2001). Note the minimal shadows and the visibility deep into the frame.

is a hallmark of horrors and film noirs, and it is used in a variety of other genres to convey <u>emotional</u> or psychological intensity.

In *Touch of Evil* (**3.59**), the shadows created by the low-key lighting underscore the murky moral terrain of the world portrayed in the film while at the same time conveying the imminent physical threat present in the scene. Similarly, in *Apocalypse Now* (1979) the theme of moral ambiguity is expressed by the lighting scheme: the chiaroscuro effect, in which darkness and light are inextricably linked, implies that the conditions of the war in Vietnam have made it impossible to separate mercy from cruelty, justice from crime, right from wrong (**3.60**).

3.59
Low-key lighting in *Touch of Evil* (1958).

3.60
Chiaroscuro and moral ambiguity: Captain Willard (Martin Sheen) in *Apocalypse Now* (1979).

Framing and Composition

In Chapter 1, we observed that story consists of all the events in a narrative, while plot is the selection and arrangement of those events as they are presented to the audience. The difference between plot and story is the difference between form and content. In order to better understand this difference, let's look at a simple analogy.

Imagine we have twelve ounces of beer and two differently shaped vessels, a long fluted glass and a mug. The beer will take the form of whichever vessel we pour it into. The content (in this case, the beer) is the same, but its appearance differs depending upon the form (the glass) in which it is presented to us.

This is a bit of an oversimplification: it isn't possible to entirely separate form from content in a work of art. But the analogy is still a useful one. In *Memento* (2000), the film's strategy of telling the story backwards is a matter of form, while the totality of the story's events is the film's content. Director Christopher Nolan could have chosen a difference narrative form (a more traditional, chronological structure, for example) for his story. Doing so, however, would have made *Memento* a completely different movie—and so for us to speak about the movie's story without taking into consideration the way in which it is told would be to ignore the essence of Nolan's film. Still, it is useful for us to isolate the film's form and ask ourselves some questions: Why did the filmmaker choose this form? How does it add to our understanding and appreciation of the film? Does the form suit the story or is it a distraction?

Just as plot determines the narrative form of a film, mise-en-scène determines its visual form. The domain of mise-en-scène is the frame. Film provides us with a frame very much like the rectangular frame of a painting or a photograph. The dimensions of that frame will vary depending upon the **aspect ratio** of the film (see Chapter 2).

As in painting and still photography, the film frame presents a particular point of view by including some objects and omitting others. It determines not just what viewers see but also how they see it. As we said at the beginning of this chapter, mise-en-scène refers not only to the elements contained in the frame—actors, objects, décor, color, shadow, and light—but the way in which they are arranged. The term for this arrangement of elements is **composition**. Every decision regarding set and costume design, lighting, acting, and cinematography affects the composition of the shot.

One important function of composition is aesthetic. Not all films have a distinctive visual style, but those that do achieve this style through composition. The way in which objects and figures are arranged and photographed determines the look of a shot. Much of the uniqueness of *Citizen Kane* is attributable to its startling mise-en-scène, which favors low-angle shots, deep focus, and diagonal arrangements that draw the viewer's eye from one top corner of the frame to the opposite lower corner. In order to achieve some of the film's extreme low-angle

3.61
Diagonal composition in *Citizen Kane*.

shots, Welles actually had openings cut in the floorboards and positioned the camera below floor level. While Welles's mise-en-scène in *Kane*, with its diagonal flow, showcases compositional imbalances (**3.61**), in *The Shining* Stanley Kubrick favors shots in which the subject is centered amid a formal geometry created by the surrounding architecture or landscape (**3.62**).

Filmmakers typically maintain a consistent style from shot to shot in order to create a sense of aesthetic unity throughout the entire film or throughout sections of the film. In *Traffic* (2000), for example, director Steven Soderbergh used various film stocks and filters to create a different color palette for each of the film's three narrative strands.

The second important function of composition is to communicate meaning. In an artistically successful film, the form suits the content. In *The Graduate*, Mike Nichols consistently opts for compositions in which something or someone obstructs the camera's view of Benjamin Braddock. This is not an arbitrary aesthetic choice. The obstruction motif underscores Benjamin's sense of himself as being hemmed in by the expectations of the older generation. In *The Cabinet of Dr. Caligari* (1920), the set

3.62
Balanced Composition in *The Shining* (1980).

design favors shadows, severe angles, curves, and jagged edges: the twisted vegetation and misshapen architecture reflect the distorted psyches of the characters. Both *The Graduate* and *Caligari* are examples of films in which the visual style coincides in a logical way with the story and its theme.

If a film's form does not suit its content, it may draw unwanted attention to itself and distract the viewer from the story. Such was the case with Spike Lee's *School Daze* (1988) for many critics such as Alan Stone, who characterized the film as "stylistically confused" and wrote that "the struggle for Black identity embodied in stereotypical characters is strangely interlaced with Hollywood production numbers a la Busby Berkley" (Stone). Similar criticism regarding stylistic inconsistency greeted Sam Mendes's *American Beauty* (1999). "For his first feature," J. Hoberman wrote in the *Village Voice*, "Mendes seems to be striving for a tricksy, overstylized naturalism without much concern for visual coherence. Bouncing from one quick fix to another, the director shifts to video-surveillance mode or cuts to an overhead angle, strews one scene with symbolic rose petals and lights another in ostentatious chiaroscuro, then, when all else fails, sneaks outside to shoot the action softcore-porn style through a rain-streaked bedroom window" (Hoberman). To return to our beer analogy for a moment, employing a style that does not suit the subject is a bit like serving ice-cold Bud Light in a teacup; the vessel isn't quite appropriate for the contents.

The means by which composition communicates meaning are subtle and somewhat ambiguous. It would be a grave mistake to assume that a particular pattern of composition means the same thing in every situation, but we can identify certain tendencies. Composition communicates by means of a spatial language. Meanings are suggested by positions of figures and objects within the frame. We can think of the frame as a hierarchical space—one in which different locations have different degrees of importance or dominance. How do we decide what is being implied or suggested by a particular composition? We can start by dividing the frame into three dimensions: height, width, and depth.

Let's begin with height. Generally speaking, the top of the frame is the dominant area. The viewer's eyes go to this part of the screen first. In addition, directors tend to fill the frame so in most shots—medium and long shots, for example—the subject's face will appear in the top half. This composition is so common that there is no point in attributing any special significance to it. But when a character appears in the lower half of the frame, it is often significant. In *The Maltese Falcon*, when Brigid O'Shaughnessy tries to manipulate Sam Spade by lying to him, she dominates the upper half of the frame, while he is relegated to the bottom left-hand portion (3.63). But when Spade turns the tables on her, the composition flips: now he occupies the top of the frame and she is in the lower right-hand corner (3.64). There is an aesthetic symmetry here (the shots neatly reverse themselves), but the composition is also conveying important information about power relationships between the two characters.

In the Thatcher Library scene in *Citizen Kane*, Walter Thatcher's statue dominates the top of the frame (3.9), emphasizing the late banker's power and influence, while the receptionist and the reporter seem to be pushed down to the bottom of the frame (3.11). The composition might be interpreted as a commentary on the impersonal and inhuman nature of power as well as a critique of class disparity in America. The lifeless personification of the wealthy banker hovers oppressively over the scene's living plebian characters, who appear to be dwarfed in comparison.

When we consider the width of the frame, or its horizontal axis, the dominant area is the center. Most compositions center the subject in the frame. Figures on the periphery of the frame tend to be diminished in importance—the sides of

3.63
In *The Maltese Falcon*, a height reversal . . .

3.64
. . . indicates a shift in the balance of power between the characters.

the frame suggest exclusion, alienation, and obscurity. In *Chasing Amy* (1997), Holden (Ben Affleck), uncomfortable and embarrassed by Alyssa's lesbianism, broods on the periphery of the frame (**3.65**), while the other characters cluster in the center. In *Eternal Sunshine of the Spotless Mind*, empty train seats occupy the center of the frame while Joel (Jim Carrey) is pushed to the far left edge of the frame, emphasizing his sense of loneliness and alienation (**3.66**). This is an example of an unbalanced composition. Directors often balance their compositions by centering the subject in the frame or by evenly distributing figures throughout the frame as in this three-shot from Ozu's *An Autumn Afternoon* (**3.38**). Directors may use a compositional imbalance to signal a psychological or emotional imbalance

3.65
An unbalanced composition emphasizes Joel's loneliness in *Eternal Sunshine of the Spotless Mind* (2004).

3.66
In *Chasing Amy* (1997), Holden (Ben Affleck) broods on the periphery of the frame.

on the part of a particular character, or an imbalance in the relationship between two or more characters, as is the case in the earlier example from *Chasing Amy*. The revelation of Alyssa's sexuality leaves Holden feeling inexperienced, insecure, and inferior; the composition captures this by locating him on the very fringes of the action in the scene.

The final frame dimension that we have to consider is depth. The film frame is a two-dimensional representation of three-dimensional space. The frame can be said to have a foreground, a mid-ground, and a background. In *Rules of the Game* (1939), the vase of callas lilies occupies the foreground, Robert speaks on the telephone in the mid-ground, and Octave enters through the door in the background (**3.67**). Depth is signaled onscreen by a variety of visual cues. The most obvious one is that objects closer to the camera appear larger than objects at a distance (note how Robert appears larger than Octave). In addition, the closer object will overlap or partially cover the object behind it, as the lilies do with Robert's figure. In a shot (**3.68**) from *The Graduate*, the figure of Mrs. Robinson in the foreground dominates the frame.

3.67

3.68

Her knee partially overlaps Benjamin, whose distance from her is signaled by his comparative diminution in size. The shot suggests Benjamin's entrapment and also comments humorously on Mrs. Robinson's intention of seducing him by positioning Benjamin's figure between her spread legs.

Movement and Color within the Frame

Just as the location of a figure within the frame is important so is its movement. Upward movements may indicate aspiration or transcendence, while a downward movement may signal a moral descent as in *Blue Velvet*, where the ominous low-angle shot of Jeffery Beaumont descending the stairs seems to echo his journey into an underworld of sex and violence (3.69). Movement toward the camera may be threatening (3.70) or seductive (3.71).

3.69
Jeffrey descends the stairs in *Blue Velvet* (1986).

3.70
Robert DeNiro moves menacingly toward the camera in *Taxi Driver* (1976).

3.71
Grace Kelly leans seductively toward the camera *in Rear Window* (1954).

3.72
A filter is used to cast a reddish light on DeNiro in *Taxi Driver*.

Color is another crucial element of mise-en-scène. Artists have used color symbolically for as long as human beings have been making art. Red, for example, has traditionally symbolized passion, whether in the form of love or anger, romance or violence. Dark browns and grays will tend to add a somber tone to a shot. Bright colors in moderation may suggest a cheerful atmosphere, but an excess of such colors can create a tone that is garish and grotesque, as in Fassbinder's *Lola* and Tim Burton's *Edward Scissorhands* (1990).

Filmmakers have at their disposal a variety of tools for bringing color into a composition. Costume, décor, and lighting may all serve as sources of color. In order to emphasize Travis's view of the city as a hellish inferno in *Taxi Driver*, Scorsese employs filters to lend some scenes a reddish tinge (3.72), while in other scenes he utilizes costumes and set design in which red dominates (3.73). In *The Departed*, the gilded dome of the Massachusetts State House represents the status and power to which Colin Sullivan (Matt Damon) aspires (3.74).

3.73
Reds predominate in costume and set design in *Taxi Driver*.

3.74
Symbolic use of color in *The Departed* (2006).

Works Cited

Benchley, Peter. *Jaws*. 1974. New York: Doubleday. New York: Fawcett, 1991.

Gibbs, John. *Mise-en-Scène: Film Style and Interpretation*. London: Wallflower, 2002.

Hoberman, J. "Boomer Bust." *Village Voice*. Village Voice, 14 Sept. 1999. Web. 3 Aug. 2010.

Lahr, John. "The Thin Man." *The New Yorker*. 14 Dec. 2005. EBSCO. Web. 3 Aug. 2010.

Maslin, Janet. "Movie Review: The Shining (1980)." *New York Times*. New York Times, 23 May 1980. Web. 3 Aug. 2010.

Toteberg, Michael. "Production Histories." Booklet. *Rainer Werner Fassbinder's BRD Trilogy*. DVD. Criterion, 2003.

Modleski, Tania. *The Women Who Knew Too Much*. 2nd ed. New York: Routledge, 2005.

Stone, Alan A. "Spike Lee: Looking Back." *Boston Review*. Boston Review, Dec. 1994/ Jan. 1995. Web. 3 Aug. 2010.

Editing

Historical Context

The earliest films did not make use of editing. The actualities produced in France, for example, by Auguste (1862–1954) and Louis (1864–1948) Lumière, such as *Workers Leaving the Factory* (1895), *Baby's Dinner* (1895), and *Arrival of a Train at La Ciotat* (1895), each consisted of a single sequence shot that ran the length of a roll of film. These brief documentaries, like the early Edison shorts, were shot on fifty-foot lengths of film and, at a speed of sixteen frames per second, ran for less than one minute.

By 1896, technological advances (specifically the Latham loop, which allowed projectors to run longer lengths of film without causing the film strip to break) had increased the length of a reel to 1,000 feet, or about sixteen minutes of running time. Filmmakers began to combine sequence shots in order to create narrative films. One of the first to do so was a compatriot of the Lumières, Georges Méliès (1861–1936). A performer and magician, Méliès was interested primarily in cinema's potential to create illusions. To this end, he employed animation, elaborate painted sets, and camera tricks such as placing a fish tank in front of the camera and filming the actors through the tank in order to create the illusion of an underwater setting.

He also made extensive use of **stop-motion photography**, which he claimed to have discovered by accident when his camera jammed and then started up again during filming; the glitch inadvertently created the illusion that a passing bus had transformed into a hearse. In his most famous film, *A Trip to the Moon* (1902), Méliès uses this technique to create the illusion of the Selenites (the alien moon-dwellers) exploding when the one of the scientists strikes them (**4.1** and **4.2**). The stop-motion process involves pausing the camera, altering the scene in some way, and then starting the camera again, creating the illusion that no time has passed between the two shots. In order to portray a magician making an elephant disappear with stop-motion, one would position the two figures in front of the camera and begin filming. The magician would wave his wand or snap his fingers. The camera would

4.1
In this stop-motion sequence, the camera is stopped and the actor leaves the frame.

4.2
A smoke bomb is set off as filming resumes, making it appear as if the alien has exploded (*A Trip to the Moon*, 1902).

stop rolling and the magician would hold his pose while the elephant was led out of the frame. Filming would them resume. The developed strip of film would make it appear as if the elephant had vanished into thin air.

While stop-motion is a cinematography technique, it is worth mentioning here because its objective is the manipulation of temporal and spatial relationships. This, of course, is also one of the primary goals of editing, and Méliès does make use of rudimentary editing in order to suggest continuity between the thirty separate scenes of *A Trip to the Moon*. He is by no means consistent on this score—at one point he makes use of overlapping shots in which, illogically, the scientists' rocket ship appears to crash into the moon twice. To a contemporary viewer, *A Trip to the Moon* is likely to appear at once sophisticated and primitive. Méliès provides striking illusions and elaborately painted sets, but he also employs a stationary camera and photographs the action as if he were recording a performance on a theater stage with the camera filming from the audience's point of view. The resulting scenes have an isolated, static quality to them which Tom Gunning attributes to Méliès' desire to showcase his special effects. "We can hardly speak of individualized characters, and the motivation of character psychology plays little role in the plot. The camera maintains the framing of a theatrical tableau, never isolating or emphasizing a character's reaction . . . The performance, sets, and theatrical tricks in this film contrast sharply with a later cinema practice of realism and transparency. Méliès flaunts his tricks and attractions; they are what the audience has come to see" (Gunning 72). The static quality of the film's scenes (or *tableaux*, as Méliès referred to them) is due in large part to the apparent lack of editing within scenes. Méliès does not cut from a long shot to a medium shot in order to better document the facial expressions of his characters, for example, nor does he change camera angles within a scene. His edits appear to be restricted to the transitions between scenes, which are accomplished with lap dissolves. (Recent investigations have revealed that Méliès did use numerous cuts and splices in each of his stop-motion shots in order to perfectly match the images, indicating that editing did occur within scenes but only in order to better disguise the nature of the camera tricks.) Despite the film's primitive nature, Méliès had, in David Cook's words, "stumbled into the narrative dimensions of the cinema" (18).

Edwin S. Porter (1870–1941) picked up where Méliès left off. With *The Great Train Robbery* (1903), Porter took the first step toward creating continuity editing and ushered in the age of narrative cinema. The film is not free of continuity errors. At one point, bandits stop a train, force all the passengers off, rob them, shoot one passenger, and then exit frame right; in the next shot they emerge from the right side of the frame and run to the left where they climb aboard the engine, creating directional confusion. Still, *The Great Train Robbery* is notable for several reasons.

First and most important, the film breaks its scenes up into shots, albeit in a crude manner. The first "scene" consists of an interior shot of the bandits entering a railroad telegraph office followed by an exterior shot of the other gang members boarding the stopped train. The next scene consists of an interior shot of the train's mail car in motion, an exterior shot atop the moving train, an exterior shot of the stopped train as the locomotive is uncoupled, an exterior shot of passengers forced off the train, an exterior shot of the bandits getting in the locomotive, an exterior shot of the bandits stopping the locomotive further down the tracks and escaping into the woods, and a shot of them mounting their horses and riding off.

Second, while it does not actually employ intercutting, *The Great Train Robbery* does imply parallel action. Unlike Méliès, Porter cuts away from scenes before they reach their dramatic conclusion and switches to another location, creating the impression that the events are occurring simultaneously. Thus, at the same time as the bandits ride off into the woods (4.3), the telegraph operator's daughter discovers her father bound and gagged (4.4). In order for this to be a true example of intercutting, Porter would have had to cut back and forth between these two scenes, which he does not do. His achievement is significant nonetheless.

Finally, while Porter's interior shots do have a staged feel still reminiscent of Méliès, the exterior shots make use of unusual camera positions and even camera movements; the exterior train shots, for example, are filmed with the camera placed at an angle to the train, and Porter uses two panning shots to follow the bandits as they escape.

D. W. Griffith (1875–1948) is responsible for consolidating and refining a variety of existing editing techniques and systematizing them into what we now think of as classical continuity editing. For example, Griffith is credited with developing the strategy referred to as **cutting in**, cutting from long shots to medium shots and close-ups in order to direct the spectator's attention to what is important in the scene. In addition to cutting in, virtually every element of classical continuity editing is present in Griffith's films.

4.3
The suggesting of parallel action . . .

4.4
. . . in *The Great Train Robbery* (1903).

Continuity Editing

Continuity editing emphasizes narrative logic over other qualities such as expressiveness. It uses an array of techniques to highlight the spatial and temporal relationships between shots, indicate causal links between events, and create a coherent and seamless narrative line. The techniques of continuity editing are so ubiquitous that most contemporary viewers take them for granted. But the strategies of continuity were not inherently obvious in the film medium at its inception; these strategies had to be developed by early filmmakers.

Let's take a very simple example: creating continuity between two different spaces. Imagine that a filmmaker with a stationary camera wants to indicate that a character sitting at a desk in one room stands up and unlocks a safe in another room. The filmmaker attempts to do this by using two shots. In the first shot, we see the man sitting at his desk and then standing up. In the second shot, we see the man unlocking a safe. Between these two shots is an ellipse, a gap in both time and space. What happened in the time between the man getting up from his chair and the moment that we see him at the safe? How much time has passed? Is he in a different room, or is this simply another part of the first room? If this is a different room, are the two rooms next to each other, or are they separated by other rooms? Are the two rooms even in the same building? In this case, rather than continuity, we have discontinuity. The gap between the two shots creates confusion on the part of viewers.

Early filmmakers such as Griffith found ways to bridge the gaps between shots and highlight the spatial, temporal, and causal links between them. Some of these strategies involved designing sets, positioning cameras, and directing actors in such a way that the action was coherent. Other strategies involved editing—piecing shots together in a manner that told a clear story. By filming a character exiting screen right in one shot and entering screen left in the next shot, a filmmaker could suggest that the two spaces were contiguous, that the second shot showed a continuation of the character's actions from the first shot, and that the two actions occurred very closely together in time. Similarly, by having a character look offscreen and then cutting immediately to a shot of an object or another person, a filmmaker could indicate what the character was looking at.

Early filmmakers learned that different editing choices led to different narrative outcomes. Let's return for a moment to our example of the man and the safe. If the man is shown in the first shot rising from his desk and walking out the door of the room, and is shown in the second shot entering the door of another room, viewers will assume that barely any time or space separate the two shots and that the room containing the safe is next door to the one with the desk. Furthermore, viewers will assume that the safe belongs to the man or that he has the authority to open it. But if we add a third shot and place it between the original two, the entire meaning of the scene changes. Imagine that after the man gets up from his desk and walks out the door of the room, we now see a shot of him lurking in the bushes outside a house and then climbing in through an open window. Then we see the shot of him entering the second room opening a safe. Now viewers will assume that the two rooms are in different locations, that some time has elapsed between the shot of the man at the desk and the shot of him in the bushes, and that he has broken into the house and the safe does not belong to him.

Elements of Classical Continuity Editing

One of the primary goals of continuity editing as it is practiced in classic Hollywood cinema is to establish, divide, and analyze space in order to focus the viewer's attention on important elements within the scene. Typically, this is accomplished by first

4.5
An exterior establishing shot of Rick's Café . . .

4.6
. . . is followed by interior establishing shot (*Casablanca*, 1942).

presenting a space in its totality, in the form of an establishing shot, and then breaking that space up into smaller units.

An **establishing shot** is typically a long or an extreme long shot that appears early in a scene and identifies for viewers the location in which the scene's action will unfold. Often a change of location is accompanied by an establishing shot that signals the new location to the audience. In *Casablanca*, the exterior shot of Rick's Café Américain at night (**4.5**) establishes the general location (and time) of the action before the camera moves inside. Once the scene moves inside the café, another establishing shot (**4.6**) defines the interior space and reveals the location of the human figures. Sometimes a series of medium shots and close-ups will be followed by another long shot in order to remind the viewer of where the figures are in the space (**4.12**). This is referred to as a **reestablishing** shot.

Once the setting is established with a long shot, the space can be broken down by cutting to medium shots and then to close-ups. In classical cinema this is often accomplished by filming a master shot as well as several additional shots. **A master shot** is a sequence (uninterrupted) shot usually filmed from long or medium distance that captures the entire scene. The master shot is augmented by medium shots (typically over-the-shoulder) and close ups, which may be filmed at the same time as the master shot if multiple camera are used or may be filmed at a different time in the case of a single camera shoot. During the editing process, the various shots are cut up and recombined. The master shot provides filmmakers with **coverage**— that is, extra footage that can be used to bridge any gaps or discontinuities in the edited footage.

In classical cinema, plot is driven by character psychology. Continuity editing divides up the space of a scene and focuses the spectator's gaze with the goal of revealing the emotions and motivations of characters and moving the plot forward. Cutting to close-ups allows a filmmaker to capture a character's emotional and psychological states as they are revealed in subtle facial expressions. In Ernst Lubitsch's *To Be or Not to Be* (1942), Maria (Carole Lombard) passes a secret message to the Polish resistance by depositing the message between the pages of a book in a bookstore. Lubitsch begins the scene with an exterior establishing shot of the location (**4.7**), and then cuts to an interior long shot that establishes the space inside the bookstore (**4.8**). He follows up this shot with a two-shot (**4.9**) of Maria and the bookseller (Wolfgang Zilzer), and from there a shot/reverse-shot sequence of medium close-ups (**4.10** and **4.11**), reducing the space to smaller and smaller units with each cut. This tightening of the frame around the characters has the effect of increasing the suspense, and psychological intensity in the scene. As Maria leaves the store and the tension subsides, there is a cut back to a reestablishing shot of the bookseller and the German soldiers (**4.12**). After the soldiers are gone, the bookseller looks inside the book for the secret message Maria has left and Lubitsch once again cuts to a medium close-up to capture the character's facial expression (**4.13**) and then an extreme close-up

4.7
To Be or Not to Be (1942).

4.8

4.9

4.10

4.11

4.12

4.13

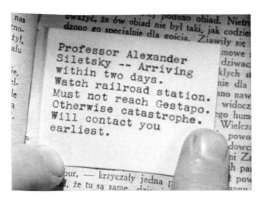

4.14

Continuity editing divides and analyzes space in *To Be or Not to Be*. Shots 4.10 and 4.11 form a shot/reverse-shot pattern.

of the message (**4.14**). Lubitsch's editing decisions direct the spectator's gaze to those elements of the scene that are important to the narrative while eliminating extraneous elements.

As we saw in our hypothetical example of the man and the safe, cuts can create discontinuity and confusion for viewers. Continuity editing deploys a number of techniques to conceal the gaps and discontinuities between shots and maintain the coherence of a space as it is divided. The most important of these is the **180-degree rule**. The technique consists of drawing an imaginary line through the scene from a bird's-eye view and insuring that the camera always remains on one side of the line during filming. In the master shot, the camera is often situated at a ninety-degree angle to the imaginary line as in camera position A. Two-shots and close-ups are photographed from various points along the arc indicated on the right side in the diagram below (**4.15**). The goal is to keep the figures in a consistent position in relation to each other. In *The Maltese Falcon*, a 180-degree line is established with Brigid O'Shaughnessy (Mary Astor) at one end of it and Sam Spade (Humphrey Bogart) at the other (**4.18** and **4.19**). The camera remains on the same side of the imaginary line throughout the various shots. Note how Spade always appears on the right side of the screen looking to the left of the frame (**4.21**) and O'Shaugnessy always appears on the left looking to the right (**4.20**), despite changes in the position of the camera. In the diagram below, once the line has been established by position A, the camera can be placed in any position to the right of the line; the placement of the camera on the left of the line (B), however, violates the 180-degree rule by crossing the line. Crossing the line will result in a shot that reverses the positions of the figures on screen, creating confusion for viewers. In the scene from *The Maltese Falcon*, notice how the windows are visible in every shot. Director John Huston never moves the camera around to the window side of the office and shoots toward the other side of the room; such a camera position would suddenly place Spade on the left side of the screen and O'Shaughnessy on the right.

When a director does cross the 180-degree line it may be to intentionally disorient the viewer or to make a thematic point. David Fincher crosses the line in a scene late in *Fight Club* (1999), in which Jack (Edward Norton) and his imaginary alter ego Tyler Dirden (Brad Pitt) suddenly switch roles. It dawns on Jack, who has up until this point been the weaker and less assertive of the pair, that since he created Tyler, he (Jack) is the one with the real control. In order to dramatize this shift in power, Fincher deliberately crosses the 180-degree line. Jack, who has appeared

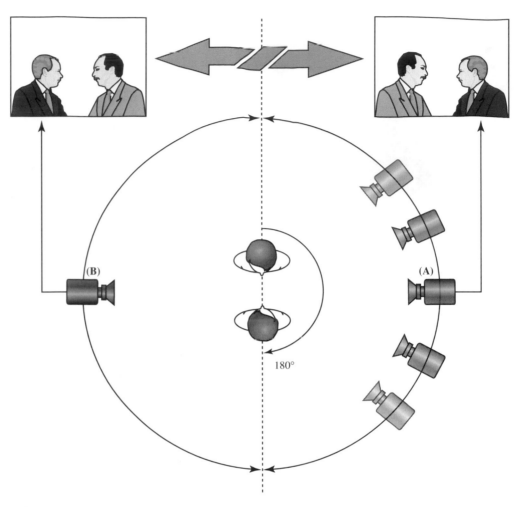

4.15
The 180-degree rule: The range of possible camera angles is represented by an imaginary circle that surrounds the action. The dotted line represents the 180-degree axis. Once the line is established with camera position A, continuity editing requires that the camera remain on one side of this axis throughout the scene. The camera positions indicated on the right are all within the limits of the rule. The camera on the left (B) violates the rule by crossing the line.

4.16
An eyeline match . . .

4.17
. . . in *The Maltese Falcon*.

4.18
The 180-degree line is established . . .

4.19
. . . and maintained.

4.20

4.21

on the right side of the screen throughout the scene (**4.22–4.27**), now suddenly appears on the left, while Tyler moves from the left side to the right (**4.25** and **4.26**). At the same time, the gun that was in Tyler's hand now appears in Jack's. The reversal is complete.

Once the 180-degree line has been established, several techniques can be used to divide and analyze the space while maintaining continuity. One of these is the **shot/reverse-shot sequence**. The initial shot shows one end of the 180-degree axis

4.22
In this scene from *Fight Club* . . .

4.23
. . . the 180-degree line is established with Tyler (Brad Pitt) on the left

4.24
. . . and Jack (Edward Norton) on the right.

4.25

4.26
The camera crosses the line . . .

4.27
. . . when the balance of power shifts from Tyler to Jack.

while the reverse-shot shows the other end. The technique is frequently used in conversations to cut back and forth between the characters as they speak. In *To Be or Not to Be*, the shots of Maria and the bookseller (**4.10** and **4.11**) form a shot/ reverse-shot pattern. Another technique for maintaining continuity is the **eyeline match**, in which a character looks off to one side of the frame and then there is a cut to another shot indicating what the character sees. In *The Maltese Falcon*, Effie (Lee Patrick) looks off screen right (**4.16**); the very next shot of Spade rolling a cigarette at his desk (**4.17**) shows us what Effie is seeing. A third technique is the **match on action**, in which two different shots of the same action are edited together in order to maintain continuity. In **4.27**, Effie rolls a cigarette for Sam and leans forward to place it in his mouth. The next shot (**4.28**) shows the continuation of this action from a different angle.

In addition to indicating spatial relationships, continuity editing enables film-makers to indicate temporal relationships. One of the objectives of continuity edit-ing is to condense time. If films had to show every event in real time, a story that takes place over a period of two months would require that the film be two months long. By eliminating unimportant action and linking together a few brief shots, a filmmaker can suggest a duration of time much longer than that actually shown on screen. In *The Graduate*, for example, Benjamin's drive from Los Angeles to Berkeley to see Elaine would have taken him over six hours in real time. The film depicts the trip with two shots of Ben driving in his car, totaling about 45 seconds of screen time.

The lap dissolve is a particularly effective way of signaling the passage of time between shots. While a **cut** joins two shots together so that the images change suddenly, a **lap dissolve** is an editing transition in which one image slowly fades

4.28
A match-on-action . . .

4.29
. . . in *The Maltese Falcon*.

out while another fades in, with the two images briefly superimposed. In *On the Waterfront*, Terry and Edie are up on the roof when he invites her to join him at a bar for a beer (**4.30**). The transition between scenes is accomplished with a lap dissolve (**4.31**). As the rooftop shot fades out, the first shot of the scene in the bar (**4.32**) fades in, indicating that a period of time has passed and that Terry and Edie are now in a new location. For a moment, the two shots appear on the screen together in superimposition. Director Elia Kazan takes advantage of the transition to visually express Terry's awakening conscience and to foreshadow his eventual redemption. Note how the rooftop television antenna in the shape of a cross appears inside Terry's head in the superimposition (**4.31**), as if he is internalizing the moral, ethical, and spiritual values represented by the symbol.

Flashbacks, in which the present flow of a story is interrupted in order to show events from the past, are often introduced with

4.30
A lap dissolve signals . . .

4.31
. . . spatial and temporal shift . . .

4.32
. . . in *On the Waterfront*.

4.33
A lap dissolve in *Casa-blanca.*

lap dissolves. *Casablanca* employs a lap dissolve to signal Rick's memory of his time together with Ilsa in Paris. The superimposition of the iconic Arc de Triomphe over the fading close-up of Rick establishes both the new location and the shift backward in time.

Another method for expressing temporal relationships is parallel editing, which makes it possible to depict two or more simultaneous events occurring in different locations. This is achieved by means of **cross-cutting** or **intercutting**— switching back and forth between shots of events taking place in multiple loca-tions. One of the earliest known examples of cross-cutting to portray parallel ac-tion occurs in Pathé's *The Runaway Horse* (1907). In the film, a milkman delivers milk inside an apartment building while outside his horse discovers a bag of oats and devours it (**4.34–4.39**). The film cuts back and forth between the action inside

4.34
Intercuttung to show parallel action . . .

4.35
. . . in *The Runaway Horse.*

4.36

4.37

4.38

4.39

the building and the action on the street four times in order to portray the simultaneous events as they occur.

The term **parallel action** to describe events occurring simultaneously in different locations is somewhat misleading. "Parallel" implies that the multiple strands of action will not converge. Very often, however, parallel actions do converge. *The Dark Knight* offers a good example. Toward the end of the film, the Joker has had District Attorney Harvey Dent (**4.40**) and his fiancée Rachel Dawes (Bruce Wayne's former girlfriend) (**4.41**) kidnapped and taken to separate ware-

4.40
The Dark Knight (2008)

4.41

4.42

4.43

4.44

4.45

4.46

4.47

houses rigged with explosives. Gordon sets off to save Dent (**4.42**), and Batman sets off to save Dawes (**4.43**). The film provides a dramatic surprise for both the audience and the characters when it ultimately reveals which strands converge and which, tragically, do not. Director Christopher Nolan plays on the established conventions of parallel action to trick the audience at the last minute when Batman kicks open the door (**4.47**) and finds not Dawes but Dent (**4.48**).

Finally, editing can affect time in a film in another way—by determining the rhythm or tempo within a scene. By in increasing the number of shots and decreasing the length of each shot, a filmmaker can create a fast tempo. Even if the action being portrayed is unfolding at a leisurely pace, the rapid cuts will give the appearance of speed. Conversely, using fewer shots of greater length will appear to slow down the action. A suspenseful fight scene such as the one that occurs between Batman and the Joker towards the end of *The Dark Knight* may use rapid cuts to create a frenetic tempo, while in *Lawrence of Arabia* (1962)

4.48

4.49

4.50

4.51

the scene depicting Lawrence's exhausting trek through the desert to rescue one of his men is composed of lingering shots.

Alternative Paradigms: Soviet Montage

The French term for editing is *montage*. Montage is also a term used to describe a particular style of filmmaking that emphasizes the expressive power of editing over other considerations such as narrative continuity or realistic action. The emphasis that the Soviet montage filmmakers placed on editing can be illustrated by the fact that the style's most iconic film, Eisenstein's *Battleship Potemkin* (1925), contained 1,346 shots. By contrast, the average total shot count for films made between 1930 and 1960, during the height of classical continuity editing, was only 300–500, according to Bordwell and Thompson (250).

In the years following the 1917 Bolshevik Revolution in Russia, Soviet filmmakers developed a style of filmmaking that built upon the editing techniques and associational strategies developed by Griffith. One of the greatest proponents of this style was the Soviet director and film theorist Sergei Eisenstein (1898–1948). Eisenstein was a Marxist and his theory of montage was based on the Marxist dialectic, in which one idea (or thesis) collides with an opposing idea (or antithesis) to produce something completely new (a synthesis). Another influence on Eisenstein was Lev Kuleshov (1899–1970). Kuleshov conducted a number of experiments on montage from which he deduced what came to be known as the "Kuleshov effect." In one of these experiments, Kuleshov took a shot of an actor's face with a neutral expression and paired it with three different shots: a bowl of soup, a girl with a teddy bear, and a dead woman in a casket. Despite the fact that the shot of the actor's face was exactly the same in each case, viewers described him as looking thoughtful when his face was intercut with the bowl of soup, smiling when it was intercut with the image of the child playing, and sad when intercut with the image of the dead woman. The implication of Kuleshov's experiment was that the juxtaposing of images creates new meanings.

Eisenstein rejected the notion of editing as merely the linking together of one shot after another in order to form a descriptive whole. "The old film-makers," he wrote, "regarded montage as a means of producing something by describing it, adding individual shots to one another like building blocks. . . . But in my view montage is not an idea composed of successive shots stuck together but an idea that DERIVES from collision between two shots that are independent of one another" (27). As a result, Eisenstein did not concern himself with verisimilitude or the appearance of realism that results from continuity editing. An example from *Battleship Potemkin* illustrates this point. The scene in which a sailor angrily smashes a plate contains overlapping action (4.52–4.55). The sailor is shown breaking same the plate twice. What's more, the two versions are different! In the first instance the sailor's right arm is raised across his body (4.54); in the second, his right arm is raised up behind him (4.55). Eisenstein is more concerned with expressing the sailor's frustration and rage than he is in factual accuracy or realism. This emphasis on expression also leads him to disregard other elements of continuity such as the 180-degree rule. The two consecutive shots of the ship's artillery guns being aimed at the headquarters of the tsarist generals in the Odessa Theater (4.66 and 4.67) are photographed from opposite sides of the 180-degree axis. Rather than a smooth transition from one shot to another, montage creates a collision between opposing shots, characterized in this case by the opposing directions of the guns.

Eisenstein's notion of montage as a collision of shots can be seen in the famous Odessa Steps scene in *Potemkin*, in which the soldiers massacre civilians. Here he juxtaposes the shots in such a way that he creates collisions between darkness and light, lines and circles, verticals and horizontals, and opposing diagonal vectors. The movement of the figures away from the camera in 4.56 contrasts with the movement toward the camera in the next shot (4.57); the two shots are literally photographed from opposing points of view. In addition, the white of the soldiers' uniforms and the building in the distance in 4.56 contrasts with the darker tones of the fleeing crowd in 4.57. The juxtaposition of the two shots

4.52

4.53

4.54

4.55

4.56

4.57

4.58

4.59

lends heightened expression to the clash unfolding onscreen. In the sequence represented by 4.58–4.61, the directional lines in the shots seem to clash with each other. In 4.58, the steps and the shadows of the soldiers create a diagonal line flowing from the upper left to the lower right of the frame, while in the next shot the fleeing crowd moves from the lower left to the upper right (4.59). Similarly, the diagonal line created by the body of the child (4.60) "collides" with the opposing diagonal created by the guns of the soldiers (4.61). In 4.62–4.65, Eisenstein juxtaposes the vertical boots of the soldier's with their horizontal

4.60

4.61

4.62

4.63

4.64

4.65

guns, and then contrasts the rigid linear (somewhat phallic) shapes of the soldiers with the softer circular forms of the woman's face and the wheels of the baby carriage. Furthermore, by varying the lengths of shots throughout the sequence on the Odessa Steps, mixing short shots with long ones, Eisenstein is able to create rhythms both within and between shots, adding an additional layer of expression. The sequence 4.68–4.77 represents an example of what Eisenstein called intellectual or ideological montage. In retaliation for the massacre on the Odessa Steps, the ship's crew members fire their artillery guns at

4.66

4.67

4.68

4.69

4.70

4.71

the generals' headquarters in the Odessa Theater (4.68). Eisenstein brackets the three overlapping shots of the theater exploding (4.72–4.74) with three very brief shots of stone angels (4.69–4.71) and three brief shots of stone lions (4.75–4.77). This montage allows him to express an abstract idea through the juxtaposition of the images. The rapid shots make it appear as if the angel is striking a blow and as if the lion is rising up, suggesting that the sailors are avenging angels and that the outraged people are finally rising up, like the lion, against tsarist oppression.

4.72

4.73

4.74

4.75

4.76

4.77

Alternative Paradigms: Deep Focus, Bazin, and Realism

As we discussed in Chapter 2, the advent of deep focus cinematography provided an alternative to classical continuity editing by allowing filmmakers to extend their shots rather than cutting. *Citizen Kane* was one of the first films to showcase the ability of deep focus to extend the length of a take. In the years immediately after World War II, the Italian Neorealists took advantage of deep focus and long takes in order to express an ideology that emphasized the struggles of the impoverished and oppressed working class. Neorealists such as Roberto Rossellini eschewed the polished techniques of classical Hollywood, despite the fact that many elements of classical cinema are apparent in films of his such as *Rome, Open City* (1945).

The French critic André Bazin argued that despite stylistic differences between Hollywood films such as *Citizen Kane* and Neorealist films *Rome, Open City* and De Sica's *Bicycle Thieves* (1948), "They are both aiming at the same results by different methods. The means used by Rossellini and De Sica are less spectacular but they are no les determined to do away with montage and to transfer to the screen the continuum of reality" (Bazin, 52). Bazin believed that deep focus and extended takes were preferable to the style of classical editing for several reasons. First, deep focus represented a heightened realism. "Deep focus brigs the viewer into a relation with the image that is closer to that which he enjoys with reality. . . . Its structure is more realistic" (50). Second, it is less controlling and oppressive than either classical editing or Soviet montage. "It implies . . . both a more active mental attitude on th part of the spectator and a more positive contribution on his part to the action in progress. While analytical montage only calls for him to follow his guide, to let his attention follow along smoothly with that of the director who will choose what he should see, here he is called upon to exercise at least a minimum of personal choice" (50). Finally, deep focus preserves the ambiguity of events, while editing interprets events and assigns meanings to them.

In *Rome, Open City*, the famous scene in which Pina is gunned down by Nazi soldiers (4.78–4.85) has a documentary-like feel to it. Whereas classical editing would call for the long shots to be intercut with numerous medium shots and close-ups to

4.78
Rome, Open City (1945).

4.79

4.80

4.81

4.82

4.83

4.84

4.85

heighten the drama of the scene, Rossellini keeps the camera at a distance during the scene's most dramatic moments, refusing to cut to close-ups that play up the emotional intensity of Pina's death.

Alternative Paradigms: Spatial and Temporal Discontinuities in Godard's Breathless

As we saw in our example of the 180-degree line being crossed in *Fight Club*, filmmakers may intentionally violate the established principles of continuity editing in order to achieve a desired effect. In the case of *Breathless* (1960), Jean-Luc Godard makes discontinuity the subject of the film. *Breathless* follows Michel Poiccard (Jean-Paul Belmondo), a petty thief who idolizes Humphrey Bogart, over a period of three days as he steals a car in Marseilles, shoots a policeman, and arrives in Paris where he tries to simultaneously elude the police and seduce Patricia Franchini (Jean Seberg). Michel and Patricia make love. She tells him she may be pregnant by another man, and Michel tries to convince her to run off with him to Italy. Ultimately, she betrays him to the police. Michel refuses to escape when he has the chance, and the police gun him down, shooting him in the back as he runs down the street. Patricia runs to his side. He makes a series of comical faces at her and then dies.

4.86
A jump cut . . .

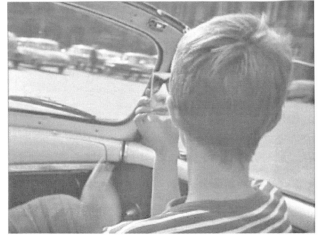

4.87
. . . .in *Breathless* (1960).

This simple plot belies the film's radical innovation. *Breathless* seems to go out of its way to keep from telling a clear, coherent story. The most obvious example of this is Godard's frequent use of jump cuts, in which a gap or ellipse is created in a shot by removing footage. The two shots of Michel and Patricia driving around Paris (**4.86** and **4.87**) are, in fact, consecutive frames in the film. By editing out the frames between, Godard creates a temporal and spatial discontinuity. Patricia's head abruptly changes position, the background is different, and it is apparent that a period of time has been skipped over, but whether it is a minute or an hour is unclear. On another occasion, a jump cut takes Patricia from one side of the street to the other.

Equally disorienting is the way in which Godard fragments events. In one scene, Michel is chased by two motorcycle cops as he drives a stolen car. When one of the cops catches up with him, Michel shoots him with a gun he's found in the glove compartment of the stolen car. In a Hollywood gangster film (of the sort Michel idealizes), this scene would be edited for maximum dramatic effect. Instead, Godard depicts the killing with just a few brief, fragmentary shots, in a manner that seems intentionally clumsy and fails to create spatial or temporal continuity (**4.88–4.95**). Godard never shows the aftermath of the shooting;

4.88

4.89

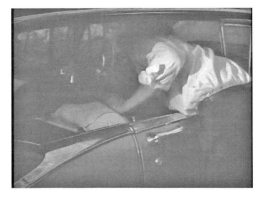

4.90

4.91

4.92

4.93

4.94

4.95

4.96

instead he cuts to a shot of Michel running across a field. In another scene, Michel arrives at the apartment of a girlfriend in Paris, and without any transition or explanation the shots inside the apartment are intercut with a brief flashback shot of Michel stealing the car in Marseilles (4.96–4.98).

By disrupting the narrative continuity and frustrating viewer expectations, Godard draws attention to the artificial conventions of classical cinema. In many ways

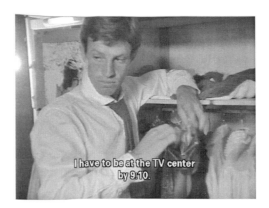

4.97

4.98

his disjointed portrayal of events is much more "real" than the professed realism that was the mainstay of Hollywood at the time. The spatial and temporal discontinuities in the narrative reflect the emotional disconnect that Michel and Patricia feel not just from each other but from themselves.

Works Cited

Bazin, André. From "What Is Film?" *Film Theory and Criticism*. 7th ed. Eds. Leo Braudy and Marshall Cohen. New York: Oxford UP, 2009, 41–53.

Bordwell, David and Kristin Thompson. *Film Art*. 9th ed. New York: McGraw-Hill, 2010.

Cook, David A. *A History of Narrative Film*. 4th ed. New York: W.W. Norton, 2004.

Gunning, Tom. "A *Trip to the Moon*." *Film Analysis*. Eds. Jeffrey Geiger and R.L. Rutsky. New York: W.W. Norton, 2005.

Eisenstein, Sergei. "The Dramaturgy of Film Form: The Dialectical Approach to Film Form." *Film Theory and Criticism*. 7th ed. Eds. Leo Braudy and Marshall Cohen. New York: Oxford UP, 2009. 23–40.

CHAPTER 5

Sound

Historical Background

The term "silent" in regards to film is somewhat misleading. From its inception, cinema was accompanied by sound. Early films were typically accompanied by live music, either from an orchestra, a piano, or a Wurlitzer organ. The notion of **synchronous sound**—sound that is recorded at the same time as the image or that occurs simultaneously with the image and appears to originate from the characters and events onscreen—was of interest to inventors very early on.

Edison and Dickson experimented with synchronous sound by pairing their Kinetograph with a phonograph prior to 1890. Such technology is referred to as **sound-on-disc** because the sound was recorded separately to a disc recorder that was synched to a camera. Film historian David Cook notes: "At the Paris World Exposition of 1900 three separate systems that synchronized phonograph recordings with film strips were exhibited" (205). Vitaphone, a sound-on-disc system developed by Western Electric, was the first synchronous sound system adopted by Hollywood. Warner Bros. employed the Vitaphone system in 1926 for the musical score of *Don Juan*. In 1927, the studio released the musical *The Jazz Singer*, which included several lines of synchronous dialogue delivered by Al Jolson. Synchronous speech had appeared prior to *The Jazz Singer* in several shorts and newsreels, but Jolson's dialogue caused a stir due to the informal context and realistic manner in which it was delivered. For this reason, *The Jazz Singer* is generally referred to as the first talking picture or "talkie."

Sound-on-film refers to a process by which sound waves are converted into light waves and photographically recorded on film alongside the images. Experiments with sound-on-film occurred as early as 1910, but the problem of amplifying the sound was not solved until the mid-1920s. By 1930, most studios were using sound-on-film rather than sound-on-disc.

The new sound technology posed several challenges. Since mixing was not yet possible, all the sounds in a scene had to be recorded simultaneously. Musical accompaniment had to be provided by a live orchestra located just offscreen. In addition, cameras had to be enclosed in clumsy soundproof booths so that the noise of the motors would not be picked up by the microphones. These booths limited the mobility of the cameras. Eventually camera booths were replaced by more mobile, lightweight blimps, and a host of other technological advances freed filmmakers from the early restrictions imposed by sound. These included the development of directional microphones, multi-track recording and mixing, and dubbing or post-synchronization, which allowed dialogue and sound effects to be recorded and synched with the image after the scene was shot.

Elements of Sound in Cinema

Speaking of his experience cutting *Alien* (1979), film editor Terry Rawlings has described what it is like to watch a film before the sound is added: "When you look at first cut of a film like *Alien* you've really got to use your imagination because there's no sound, for one thing. Lots of those scenes were shot with all these noisy machines or effects working on the stages so you used to run all these things silent. You sit there and look at him [Harry Dean Stanton] creeping around in the rain room silent and it's boring".

Rawling's remarks point out just how important sound is to creating the world of a film. A movie doesn't really come to life until the various sound elements—dialogue, ambient noises, Foley effects, musical score—are added and mixed. These elements may be used to reveal character psychology, create a mood, convey plot, foreshadow events, delineate space, and indicate time.

There are three types of film sound: speech, noise and music. Each of these elements may be used diegetically or nondiegetically. As you will recall from Chapter 1, a diegetic film element is one that exists inside the world of the story. In *Casablanca*, the version of "You Must Remember This" played by Sam is diegetic, but the orchestral strings that accompany Rick's late-night meeting with Ilsa in his room above the café are nondiegetic. In the latter scene, the café is closed, the band has gone home, and Rick and Ilsa are alone. The music we hear exists outside the world of the story. Sound effects usually emanate from within the story, such as Walter Neff's footsteps as he walks down a dark street in *Double Indemnity*. But non-diegetic sound effects, such as the distorted animal noises that accompany the scenes of sexual violence in David Lynch's *Blue Velvet* (1986), may be used for the specific meanings associated with them. Often a scene contains a combination of diegetic and non-diegetic sounds. In *Oldboy*, the extensive montage of Oh Dae-Su's imprisonment is constructed with several layers of sound. Oh Dae-Su's voiceover and the sounds from the television are diegetic, but the music and the faint but persistent ticking of a clock are nondiegetic (there is no clock in Oh Dae-Su's room).

Sounds are characterized by their volume, pitch, and timbre. **Volume** refers to how loud a sound is. By manipulating the volume of particular sounds, filmmakers can convey information about characters or elicit responses in viewers. A character's anger or fear may be indicated by a raised voice, while sadness or depression may be indicated by soft tones. In a quiet scene, any loud sudden noise is likely to startle audiences and make them jump in their seats. Horror films employ this technique so frequently that it is virtually a cliché. Often the source of the startling noise is harmless, causing audience members to laugh nervously and relax just enough to be caught off guard when the real monster appears moments later. The popular technique is sometimes referred to in the industry as a "bus" after the scene in *Cat People* (1942) in which it was first used. That scene is an excellent example of how volume and rhythm can be used to control the mood of a scene. Alice is walking

5.1
Brett (Harry Dean Stanton), Ripley (Sigourney Weaver), and Parker (Yaphet Koto) hunt for the alien creature in *Alien* (1979).

home through Central Park at night. She is being followed by Irena. The alternating staccato rhythms of the two women's high heels clicking on the pavement create a sense of tension and anticipation. The footsteps grow louder and more pronounced as the scene progresses. When the sound of Irena's footsteps suddenly ceases, it becomes apparent that she has transformed into a panther and is about to attack Alice. Alice senses that she is being stalked; the rapidly increasing rhythm of her footsteps as she tries to escape conveys her growing anxiety as well as that of the audience. At the moment of greatest suspense, there is a loud growl (of either a panther or an engine) and a bus suddenly pulls up in front of Alice, its brakes hissing loudly like an enormous cat. The audience is first startled and then relieved.

Alien actually resorts to using a "bus" on several occasions, two of them involving Jones the cat. In the first incident, the soft pulsing of the ship's engines, the low beeping of the tracking device, and the hushed whispers of Ripley, Parker, and Brett as they hunt for the alien creature (**5.1**, **5.2**, and **5.3**) create a quietly tense background against which the sudden shrieking of the cat (**5.4**) is both shocking and

5.2
The tense, hushed quality of the scene, achieved through whispered dialogue, soft footsteps, and the low electronic beeping sounds of the equipment . . .

5.3
. . . is suddenly shattered . . .

5.4
. . . by the high-pitched screeching of Jones the cat.

terrifying. Brett seems to express the sense of relief on the part of the audience when he says to a panicky Parker, "It's the cat, man." Later in the film, Ripley finds herself alone on the ship's navigation deck, papers fluttering softly in the breeze from a nearby fan. The scene is accompanied by a hauntingly ethereal musical score featuring woodwinds and strings. Once again, the high-pitched screech of the cat disrupts the hushed tone of the scene and startles both character and audience.

Pitch refers to the acoustic frequency of a sound and is characterized as high or low. A bass is on the low end of the scale, while a soprano is on the high end. Low-pitched sounds tend to signal power, authority, and menace as in the deep bass of Darth Vader's voice. High-pitched sounds often convey helplessness or panic; when they occur suddenly these sounds have a startling and unsettling effect on the listener as in case of the screeching cat in *Alien*, the hissing bus in *Cat People*, or the high-pitched violins that accompany the shower scene in *Psycho*.

Timbre is a vaguely defined term that refers to the quality or tone of a sound. If an alto saxophone and a trumpet are played at the same volume and pitch, the difference in timbre is what allows a listener to distinguish between the two instruments. Timbre also enables us to tell apart voices that may have the same pitch.

Speech

Speech consists of dialogue (the words spoken by the characters), but it also includes other human sounds, such as laughter, sighing, moaning, and crying. When these words and sounds originate with the characters in the film, as is usually the case, they are diegetic. Sometimes a character's voice will speak directly to the audience from a time or place that is not synchronized with the image. In *Out of the Past*, Jeff Bailey's voice narrates a flashback sequence. He is speaking from inside a car in the present tense, but the action unfolding onscreen takes place in the past. This is known as a **voiceover**. Voiceover dialogue spoken by a character in the film is diegetic because it originates from inside the story. However, voiceover dialogue spoken by a character outside the world of the story—for example, an omniscient narrator such as the one in Woody Allen's *Vicky Christina Barcelona* (2008)—is nondiegetic.

Dialogue always has a **text**. The text consists of the actual words spoken by the character and the explicit or apparent meaning attached to them. Often dialogue has a **subtext** as well, an implied meaning that lies beneath the surface of what the character is saying. A dialogue's subtext is determined to some degree by its **context**—the circumstances in which the dialogue is spoken.

In order to illustrate the relationship between text, subtext, and context, let's look at a simple example. Imagine that two female characters in their mid-thirties, Alexis and Nicole, step out onto a beautiful tropical beach. "God," Nicole says, "it's *hot* out here." In the limited context of the scene, we have only the text of the dialogue to go on. The explicit meaning of Nicole's comment is that the weather is hot. However, if the context of the dialogue is altered, a subtext may emerge. Imagine that Alexis and Nicole have each recently gotten divorced, have decided to take a vacation together at a singles resort, and that the tropical beach is occupied by handsome men in skimpy bathing suits. Nicole's comment now has a second possible meaning (a subtext) attached to it—one that refers not just to the weather, but to the attractive men on the beach.

Subtextual dialogue adds layers of psychological complexity to characters and captures the way in which people communicate in real life. For a variety of reasons, most of us don't come right out and say exactly what we mean. Perhaps we fear negative repercussions, or we're trying to protect another person's feelings. Subtextual dialogue represents a struggle between what a character is really feeling and what he allows himself to express; it reveals a character's complex psychology by capturing his or her conflicting impulses.

In *Rear Window* (1954), the complicated relationship between Jeff and Lisa is conveyed through the subtext of their dialogue. The context is that Lisa says she loves Jeff and wants to marry him, while Jeff feels they are incompatible. In one of the film's early scenes, Lisa arrives at Jeff's apartment wearing an expensive evening gown.

JEFF: Is this the Lisa Fremont who never wears the same dress twice?
LISA: Only because it's expected of her . . . right off the Paris plane. Think it will sell?
JEFF: Depends on the quote—Let's see, there's the plane ticket over, import duties, hidden taxes, profit markups—
LISA: A steal at eleven hundred dollars.
JEFF: Eleven hundred dollars! They ought to list that thing on the stock exchange.
LISA: We sell a dozen a day in this price range.

JEFF:	Who buys them? Tax collectors?
LISA:	Even if I had to pay, it would be worth it . . . just for the occasion.
JEFF:	Something big going on somewhere?
LISA:	Going on right here. It's a big night.
JEFF:	It's just a run-of-the-mill Monday. Calendar's full of them.
LISA:	It's opening night of the last depressing week of L.B. Jefferies in a cast.
JEFF:	Hasn't been any big demand for tickets.
LISA:	That's because I bought out the house. This cigarette box has seen better days.
JEFF:	Oh, I picked that up in Shanghai—which has also seen better days.
LISA:	It's cracked—and you never use it. And it's too ornate. I'm sending you up a plain, flat silver one—with just your initials engraved.
JEFF:	Now that's no way to spend your hard-earned money.
LISA:	But I want to, Jeff.

The text of Lisa's and Jeff's dialogue is fairly innocuous. They are talking about Lisa's dress and Jeff's cigarette box, but beneath the surface, at the subtextual level, the two are discussing their relationship and their conflicting feelings about each other. While Jeff is attracted to Lisa's beauty and sophistication (as she slyly points out, such qualities are "expected of her"), he also appears to be somewhat intimidated by it. His incredulity at the price of her dress reveals both his feelings of inadequacy and his sense that he and Lisa are incompatible. She tries to remain upbeat and positive ("It's a big night"), while Jeff contradicts her at every step ("It's just a run-of-the-mill Monday. Calendar's full of them"). By the end of the conversation, the exchange over the cigarette box seems to sum up their relationship. Lisa is offering him something precious (the silver cigarette box and, by implication, herself). Jeff's explicit rejection of the former ("that's no way to spend your hard-earned money") implies a rejection of the latter. Lisa's desire to replace Jeff's gaudy and battered cigarette box with something sleeker and more fashionable also hints at another aspect of her feelings for him—her desire not just to marry him, but to change him, to transform him into someone both more settled and more sophisticated. She avoids coming out and directly stating these feelings because she knows Jeff will react negatively to them, so she projects her feelings onto a trivial object, the cigarette box, just as Jeff projects his reservations about Lisa onto her dress.

Noise

Filmmakers often use layers of sound to create a fully imagined environment. In *Alien*, Ridley Scott employed a sound palette that consisted of human speech, a musical score that utilized several exotic instruments such as the didgeridoo, and an array of **noises** corresponding to the engines, instruments, and mechanical systems of the *Nostromo* as well as to the actions of its human, android, and alien passengers. Terry Rawlings has spoken about how challenging it was to edit the film because so much of the original footage was completely silent. The noise generated on the set by the machinery used to create many of the special effects made it necessary to shoot without sound. In the scene in which Brett searches for Jones the cat and encounters the alien in the "rain room," all the subtle ambient noises—the dripping of the water, the jingling of the chains—that contribute to the scene's unbearable buildup of suspense are the result of sound effects added to the film in postproduction.

Sound effects can transform a plastic prop into a realistic piece of equipment or make a set constructed out of scrap metal seem like a functioning spacecraft. When Sigourney Weaver slips a prop space helmet over her head late in the film, a simple air-lock sound effect is used to create the illusion that the prop is a functioning piece of high-tech equipment.

Technicians record some sounds specifically for a film and use stock recordings to create other noises (the "Wilhelm scream", for example, first recorded in 1951, has reportedly been used in over 200 films). **Foley artists**, named after sound artist Jack Foley, are specialists who create realistic sound effects—such as swords clashing, a face being punched, or footsteps slogging through mud—that are perfectly synchronized with the actions depicted in the film footage. The sounds are created in a Foley studio in real time as the film is screened.

The degree to which a sound is realistic or faithful to its visual source is referred to as **fidelity**. Most of the time, sound fidelity is desirable. Typically, when a gun goes off in a film we want to hear something that sounds like a gunshot, not like a car horn or a braying donkey.

But there are occasions in which a sound lacking in verisimilitude can add important layers of meaning to a story by functioning symbolically. In *Alien*, the ship's computer is nicknamed "Mother," the set design's tubular structures and womb-like spaces suggest the female reproductive system, and the bloody emergence of the infant alien from Kane's chest suggests a traumatic birth scene. Ridley Scott recalls that sound editor Jim Shields used an organic pulsing sound, possibly a heartbeat, to create the ambient sound effect for the *Nostromo*'s engines. The choice to use an organic sound to depict a mechanical function serves to identify the ship with the human body and underscores what Barbara Creed has identified as the film's theme of "the monstrous-feminine as archaic mother" (16). By assigning a heartbeat to the ship rather than a more realistic mechanical noise, Shields highlights this theme in the film.

A more obvious example of symbolic sound occurs in *Run Lola Run* (1998), where the sound of a phone receiver dropping into its cradle is replaced by a heavy metallic thud that recalls the sound of a cell door slamming shut. This nondiegetic sound effect emphasizes the seriousness of Manni's situation and the weight of the burden that's been placed on Lola's shoulders. It also conveys the sense of the characters as trapped, imprisoned by fate and circumstances.

Sound does not have to lack fidelity in order to serve a symbolic function. Realistic sound effects can also be used to add layers of meaning to the action onscreen. In *The Marriage of Maria Braun* (1979), recordings of actual radio broadcasts form a backdrop to several scenes, emphasizing the degree to which public events, such as the war, intrude on private lives. In the film's final tragic scene involving Maria and Hans, the broadcast of West Germany's victory over Hungary in the 1954 World Cup final underscores the degree to which even intimate personal relationships in postwar Germany have become competitions or power struggles.

Music

We saw how the increasing rhythm of a seemingly mundane noise, such as Alice's footsteps in *Cat People*, can indicate a character's fear and anxiety and instill in the viewer a rising sense of tension and suspense. **Music** can be even more effective than noise at controlling the mood and pace of a scene.

In *City of God* (2002), the brisk pace of the opening scene is created by a combination of rapid cuts, a frenetic samba, and the sound of a knife being sharpened (5.5). The music in the early shots is diegetic: we can see the street musicians playing guitars, cavaquinhos, and traditional Brazilian percussion instruments (5.6). The scene is a street barbecue in a Rio de Janeiro slum. Chickens are being slaughtered, plucked, and cooked. One bird stands off to the side nervously awaiting its fate (5.7). The samba, in combination with the rhythmic sharpening of the knife and chopping of vegetables (5.8), creates a sense of mounting tension as the audience waits to see what will become of the chicken. When the bird escapes (5.9), the drama is intensified by an abrupt pause in the music and the gang leader Li'l Zé shouts, "Get that chicken, man!" (5.10). A chase ensues through the narrow alleyways. When the music starts up again, it is nondiegetic and purely percussive, echoing the gunshots of the gang members as they shoot at the chicken (5.11). The camera then cuts to Rocket, who is walking down the street with Stringy (5.12). Stringy tells him, "If Li'l Zé catches you, he'll kill you." The use here of a single extended shot and the conspicuous lack of musical accompaniment establishes a contrast between the calm, grounded Rocket and the unstable, unpredictable Li'l Zé. The lack of music also links Rocket to the chicken, whose attempts to escape the gang members parallel Rocket's efforts to escape the *favela*.

5.5
In *City of God* (2002), the rhythmic sound of a knife being sharpened . . .

5.6
. . . in combination with diegetic samba music sets the pace for the rapid cuts.

5.7
A chicken looks on . . .

5.8
. . . as the rhythmic chopping of a knife foreshadows the bird's fate.

PRODUÇÃO **ANDREA BARATA RIBEIRO** E **MAURÍCIO ANDRADE RAMOS**

5.9
At the moment the chicken escapes, the music abruptly ceases.

5.10
L'il Zé orders his gang
to catch the chicken . . .

5.11
. . . and nondiegetic
music consisting
exclusively of frenetic
percussion accompa-
nies the chase.

5.12
When we cut to Rocket
(left) walking on an
adjacent street, the lack
of musical accompani-
ment recalls the ear-
lier shot of the chicken
trying to escape from
Li'l Zé's gang.

The expressive qualities of music also make it ideal for rendering subtle mood shifts in characters. In *Taxi Driver*, Bernard Hermann's jazz score alternates between a martial theme and a lyrical romantic theme. The martial theme with its snare drums recalls Travis's tour in Vietnam and foreshadows his violent behavior later in the film, while the romantic passages express his loneliness and his desperate attempts to connect with women. The dual aspect of the score echoes the split in Travis's personality.

Space and Time

In cinema, sound helps to create and define space in a variety of ways. One of the most obvious examples of sound being used to define space is employed by Steven Spielberg in both *Jaws* and *Saving Private Ryan* (1998). In both films, Spielberg employs the technique of muffling or muting the sound when the camera slips underwater in order to approximate the aural effect of being submerged; when the camera rises above the surface, the mute is removed and the sound returns to full volume and clarity.

5.13
In *Jaws* (1975), a change in environment . . .

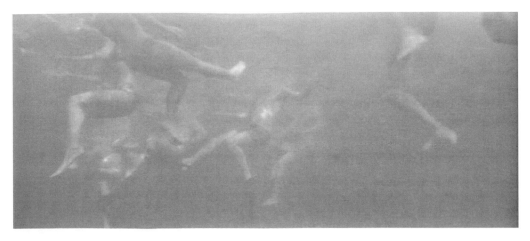

5.14
. . . is accompanied by a change in sound.

Such aural cues are so common in films that we often take them for granted. Distance and direction, for example, are signaled by volume. The sound of a nearby person or object will be louder than the sound of a person or object off in the distance. An approaching sound will increase in volume, while a retreating sound will decrease. Large, cavernous spaces can be suggested by adding reverb in postproduction, which creates an echo effect. Offscreen sound indicates space outside the frame in which action is occurring.

By assigning different musical themes to different locations, filmmakers can distinguish among various types of spaces and create a distinct mood and set of thematic associations for each. In *On the Waterfront*, the deafening drums and blaring brass that accompany scenes set on the streets and docks suggest the harshness and brutality of the characters' day-to-day struggles to survive in the city, while ethereal harp chords identify the rooftops as a place of contemplation and refuge.

In addition to indicating space, sound can signal time. We've already seen how sound can establish a relationship between the past and the present in a voiceover. Sometimes a filmmaker will use a sound as a transition between scenes that occur

5.15
COSTELLO: When you're facing a loaded gun, what's the difference? (*The Departed*, 2006).

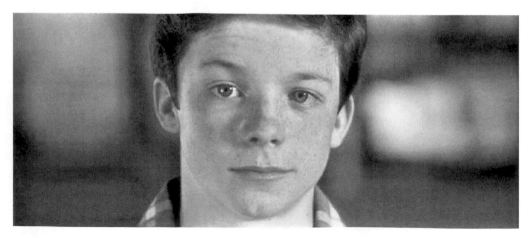

5.16
Young Colin.

5.17
COSTELLO (V.O.): That's my boy.

at different times by employing a **sound bridge**. By overlapping a sound from one scene to another, events can be logically linked together. In *The Departed* (2006), Frank Costello (Jack Nicholson) lectures a young Colin Sullivan (Conor Donovan) on moral relativism inside a dim auto repair garage. "When I was your age they would say we could become cops or criminals," Frank tells Colin. "Today what I'm saying to you is this: When you're facing a loaded gun, what's the difference?" The camera cuts from a close-up of Frank (**5.15**) to a close-up of young Colin (**5.16**). Then there is another cut to a close-up of an adult Colin (Matt Damon) wearing a Massachusetts State Police uniform (**5.17**). Frank's voice overlaps from the previous scene: "That's my boy." The sound bridge stitches together past and present. It makes clear that the boy we were just looking at (Donovan) is now the man before us (Damon). It also suggests what has transpired in the years between the two shots by indicating that Costello the gangster now owns Sullivan the cop.

Writing about Film

Types of Writing

Different viewers watch films in different ways and often for very different reasons. Some people watch a film simply hoping to be entertained for a couple of hours. Others look at films as cultural and historical artifacts that reveal important insights into the society that has produced them and that often raise intriguing philosophical questions. Still others are interested primarily in the aesthetic or technical aspects of a film—the way in which the film expresses itself. It's possible, for example, to watch *The Dark Knight* for no other reason than to admire Heath Ledger's virtuoso performance as The Joker, enjoy the twists and turns of the plot, and revel in the action sequences. But it's equally possible to find the plot implausible and Ledger's performance a bit over-the-top, yet still be fascinated by the film as an expression of American angst and ambivalence about the appropriate use of surveillance and military power in a post-9/11 world.

Just as there are a variety of ways in which to watch films, there are also a number of different ways in which to write about them. These range from informal user comments posted on websites such as Amazon or Netflix to academic books or articles on esoteric topics in film studies. Each type of writing has its appropriate tone and format, and each is aimed at a particular audience. Some of these audiences are broader than others. While a film review appearing on the website of a mainstream newspaper is written to appeal to the general population, which includes readers with diverse interests and varying levels of knowledge, an article on fetishistic scopophilia in Hitchcock's *Rear Window* published in an academic journal is likely be of interest to only a relatively small audience of scholars interested in spectatorship theory and film.

There are four types of writing about film that are relevant to our discussion:

1. Informal writing intended for an audience
2. Screening notes
3. Film review writing
4. Academic writing

Texts, Tweets, and Online Discussion Posts: Writing Informally for an Audience

Technological advances have provided individuals with virtually unlimited opportunities to put their thoughts and opinions about films into writing and share them with others. If you've ever come out of a theater and fired off a text message to a friend praising or trashing the movie you just saw, then you've engaged in a form of writing about film. And if you've ever gone to Amazon.com or Netflix.com and read the user reviews of a particular DVD, then you have read the opinions of amateur film reviewers.

The quality of such writing can vary widely. Some individuals writing in informal venues such as these go to great pains to develop well-reasoned and adequately supported arguments. But more often than not, writers in this situation adopt a colloquial style (one very similar to the way they speak) and don't concern themselves much with organization or structure. The primary goal of such writing is to express an opinion in as brief a form as possible. After all, a text message is currently limited to 160 characters and a Twitter post to 140. Even in cases where writers have plenty of space, the form seems to beg for brevity: readers surfing the Netflix site looking for a DVD recommendation are unlikely to want to read a six-paragraph essay complete with an introduction and a conclusion. It's not uncommon to read a DVD review on a website or a text message from a friend that states simply: "This film sucked. Boring, boring, boring. Don't waste your money."

On the one hand, this is a fairly efficient bit of writing; it tells you exactly how the writer feels and what her recommendation is regarding the film. Ultimately, however, this sweeping dismissal of a film isn't very useful to a reader because it lacks specifics. We never learn what criteria the writer is applying to her evaluation. Why did the film "suck"? What made it boring? Maybe the movie in question is a quirky independent drama and the reviewer is primarily a fan of blockbuster action films, in which case we might take her criticism with a grain of salt. If we knew the specific reasons why the reviewer didn't like the film, we could make an informed decision about whether or not to take her advice.

While the informal tone and loose structure of such writing is not appropriate for a formal academic paper, you may on occasion find yourself asked to write informally in the context of the film studies classroom. For example, your instructor may require you to post comments to an online bulletin board or discussion group. While the standards for such an assignment are not as rigorous as they are for a formal paper, keep in mind that effective writing is effective writing no matter what the venue. Try to make a habit of explaining and supporting your opinions even when you are posting to an online discussion or texting your review of a film to a friend. This will get you in the habit of supporting your opinion with specific evidence.

Screening Notes

Note-taking is a type of informal writing in which the writer is the intended audience. Whether you are preparing to write a review for your college newspaper, participate in a discussion in a film class, or write an academic essay to fulfill a class assignment, it can be difficult to remember important details about a film after you've seen it. For this reason, it's important to get in the habit of taking notes during screenings.

Your **screening notes** should consist of your initial impressions, opinions, and observations about the film, including your thoughts on the film's narrative structure, mise-en-scène, cinematography, editing, and sound. Your notes might include observations about motifs, transcriptions of important bits of dialogue, or sketches to remind you of particular shot compositions. You might note, for example, that water appears often and in various forms in *The Graduate*; that characters in *The Searchers* frequently appear framed in doorways, cave openings, or other entryways; or that Father Barry makes a direct comparison between Dugan's death and Christ's crucifixion in *On the Waterfront*. Don't worry too much yet about what these things might mean; you can come up with an interpretation later. You also needn't concern yourself with organizing your thoughts or focusing on a main point; this is just the information gathering stage of the writing process. Of course, if any theories or interpretations do pop into your head while you're watching the film, be sure to jot them down.

Remember, your ultimate goal when taking screening notes is to record observations from which you can later develop a thesis and gather evidence to support whatever argument you make. Use the Screening Notes Checklist shown later in this chapter as your guide to what to pay attention to when making notes.

Film Reviews

Unlike screening notes or many online discussion group posts, the **film review** is a structured piece of writing. It consists of a plot summary, a thesis statement (usually a recommendation regarding whether the film is worth seeing), some supporting points, and a conclusion. Because the review is aimed at prospective moviegoers, reviewers are careful not to include spoilers—plot revelations that may give away a film's ending, reveal a shocking twist, or otherwise diminish a viewer's enjoyment of the movie.

A review is intended for a general audience, and its primary purpose is to make a recommendation about the film in question. Is the film worth seeing? The answer to this question provides the review with its thesis or main point. The writer will then go on to briefly support his assessment of the film with some examples. Often these examples are not very specific—both because reviewers don't want to give away too much of a movie's plot and because film reviews are intended to be brief.

In his review of *Blue Velvet*, Roger Ebert's main point or thesis was as follows: "*Blue Velvet* contains scenes of such raw emotional energy that it's easy to understand why some critics have hailed it as a masterpiece . . . And yet those very scenes of stark sexual despair are the tipoff to what's wrong with the movie. They're so strong that they deserve to be in a movie that is sincere, honest and true. But *Blue Velvet* surrounds them with a story that's marred by sophomoric satire and cheap shots." But when it comes to supporting this point with specific examples, Ebert doesn't go into much more detail than to comment that "Everyday town life is depicted with a deadpan irony; characters use lines with corny double meanings and solemnly recite platitudes."

Readers accept this sort of generalization from reviewers, but the student writing a paper for a film class will be expected to support his opinions in more detail. It's also important to note that the judgments rendered in film reviews regarding the quality of the acting or the level of excitement generated by the plot are not really appropriate in an academic essay.

Academic Writing

Academic writing includes critical essays and theoretical writing.

Theoretical writing on cinema is done primarily by film scholars or those from other disciplines such as philosophy, history, or psychology. Such writing may examine topics such as whether film is a language and if so how that language functions; the relationship between cinema and ideology; the relationship between cinema and the spectator; or the influences of social, political, and economic forces on the film industry. Film theory presents complex material and often requires that readers have an extensive knowledge of film history and other topics such as psychoanalysis, Marxism, and feminist theory. The tone of such writing can seem both formal and aloof. Film theorists are writing for an audience that shares their expert knowledge of the field and of the field's sometimes confusing terminology; they don't pause to explain concepts that may be confusing to the uninitiated.

The type of paper students are required to write most frequently in a film studies class is the **critical essay**. Such writing is academic in that its concerns are scholarly. A critical essay does not focus on the issue of whether a film is good or bad the way a film review does. Rather, it addresses some of the same issues as the theoretical essay but from a less complex and more accessible point of view. A critical essay may explore the theme of redemption in *On the Waterfront*, the use of the water motif in *The Graduate*, the way in which Godard uses editing techniques to frustrate viewer expectations in *Breathless*, or the way in which *The Dark Knight* is influenced by American policies in the wake of 9/11.

The tone of a critical essay is more formal than that of a film review. Avoid using the first person ("I") or second person ("you"). Typically, critical essays make use of technical terms such as those mentioned in previous chapters. Write as if your audience is your instructor or a very knowledgeable fellow student. Assume that your readers have at least the same level of film knowledge as you have. Also imagine that you don't know your readers personally and that you want to make a good impression on them. Avoid slang and inappropriate language. Explain your points clearly and thoroughly.

The Writing Process

Writing is a process, and as such it is best approached in three stages: **prewriting, writing,** and **revision.** Taking shortcuts, such as skipping the prewriting stage, is likely to cost you additional time and work rather than make you more efficient.

Let's use grocery shopping as a rough analogy. Like writing, grocery shopping is an activity that many people find stressful and unpleasant. If you're one of those people, your goal is to get it over with as quickly and painlessly as possible. Making a grocery list before you leave the house may strike you as a waste of time, an unnecessary task that merely prolongs an already unpleasant activity. You'll decide what you need when you get to the store; it'll be quicker that way.

When you arrive at the supermarket, you grab a shopping cart and make your way up and down the aisles, picking items off the shelves and tossing them into your cart as they catch your eye. You pick up butter and eggs in the dairy aisle and the thought of breakfast makes you think of coffee so, before you forget, you head over to the coffee aisle to get a couple of pounds of French roast—which reminds you that you forgot to pick up milk. So it's back to the dairy aisle. The milk makes you think of tea and you remember that you used the last of the Earl Grey to brew a pot last night, so you make your way back to the coffee aisle to pick up the tea bags.

You get the idea. At this rate, you'll retrace your steps several times instead of getting everything you need on a single trip down each aisle. This is an utterly inefficient way to food shop. In fact, you will have wasted far more time than it would have taken you to simply make a list of what you needed.

The prewriting phase is roughly equivalent to making a grocery list before you start writing. If you skip this part of the process, you're likely to end up with a disorganized essay that will take you longer to write and will require many more revisions than it would have had you just spent a little bit of time organizing your thoughts beforehand.

Prewriting

The prewriting process begins with your screening notes. Detailed notes about the film will make it easier for you to brainstorm an idea for your paper and to support that idea with examples. If you are viewing a film on a DVD player at home, you have the option of pausing and replaying portions of it, which will make the note-taking process easier. If you're viewing the film in class, it may be a bit more challenging.

When you watch a film for the first time, it's a good idea to jot down anything that catches your attention. Pay attention to unusual camera angles or striking elements of the mise-en-scène and make note of them. Keep a copy of the Screening Notes Checklist handy so that you can refer to it. Don't worry too much about formulating an interpretation of what you see: there will be time for that after you've watched the entire film, looked over your notes, and done some brainstorming.

Brainstorming

Before you start writing your essay, you need to know what you're going to write about. To return to our grocery shopping analogy, if you don't know what you're going to cook, you won't know what to put on your shopping list. Without a specific recipe in mind, you're likely to return from the store with a bunch of disparate ingredients that don't add up to a meal. In the case of your essay, it isn't enough to say you are going to write about a particular movie. You need to know what you want to say about that movie. You need a **thesis.**

What is a thesis? A thesis is an opinion, which you will prove over the course of your essay. A factual statement is not a thesis. You can't write an essay, for example, in which you argue that *On the Waterfront* is about a dockworker named Terry Malloy. That observation is self-evident from the film and therefore cannot form the basis of an argument. If you try to base a paper on this idea, what you will wind up with instead is a plot summary. However, if you were to argue that in *On the Waterfront* Terry Malloy is redeemed through violence, you would have the basis for an interesting essay. One way to test whether a statement is a fact or an opinion is to ask whether one might reasonably argue the opposite point of view. In the case of our first statement, the opposite point of view—"*On the Waterfront* is not about a dockworker named Terry Malloy"—is nonsensical: proving it would require that one completely ignore the plot of the movie, and the resulting argument would not elucidate the film in any way. With our second statement, however, one could reasonably take an opposing point of view and argue that Terry is not redeemed through violence—in this case, one might argue that Terry is redeemed by Edie's love, or perhaps that he isn't redeemed at all.

The purpose of your essay is to establish a thesis and support it with evidence from one or more films. How do you develop a thesis about a film? There is no simple answer to this question. Developing a thesis is for many students the most challenging part of writing a paper. The process—which we will refer to as brainstorming—involves looking back over your screening notes and identifying a pattern that will enable you to draw some conclusions about the film.

Pattern: Repetition and Variation

By a **pattern**, we mean a repeated form. In the arts, such repeated elements are referred to as **motifs**. If an element appears once in a film, we are likely to overlook it. But when a form or an image occurs more than once, it draws our attention. If such images are carefully chosen they can convey important information about the film's theme or underlying meaning. In *On the Waterfront*, fences serve as a motif: they appear over and over again in the film. An observant student will indicate this the prominence of this motif in her screening notes. But how can she determine what it means?

It's important to keep in mind that an interpretation is always a matter of opinion. There is no right or wrong interpretation of a particular motif's meaning. There are, however, plausible and implausible interpretations. It would be implausible, for example, to suggest that the fences represent Terry's desire to take up the sport of fencing. First of all, there is no clear connection between fences and fencing; second, the sport of fencing has nothing to do with the story, which concerns dockworkers, mobsters, and union corruption on the New York City waterfront in the early 1950s.

Finally, even if you could make such an argument, what possible light would it shed on the film? The answer is, none.

We can, however, start to arrive at a more plausible interpretation of the fence motif in the film by asking ourselves some relevant questions. What is the purpose of a fence? How does this purpose relate to the circumstances of the characters in the film? Which characters appear in scenes with fences, and where are they positioned in relation to these fences?

Fences are meant either to enclose and imprison or to keep out. *On the Waterfront* is a film about characters who are trapped or imprisoned by social and economic circumstances; at the same time, they are excluded from the American dream. Therefore, the fence motif may be said to represent their predicament by implying both imprisonment and exclusion. The fact that the fences are a ubiquitous aspect of the film's setting suggests that the forces oppressing these characters are inextricably woven into the fabric of American society. Other meanings are also possible. On several occasions in the film, Terry appears behind a fence, including several scenes in which he is shown inside a pigeon coop. Such shots emphasize his bestial nature—and, in fact, Edie describes Terry's way of life as "living like an animal." These shots of Terry inside the pigeon coop also serve to link him to the pigeons, which are identified in the film with the victimized dockworkers. As this example indicates, a single motif may have several connotations. A film may contain a number of motifs. In addition to fences, *On the Waterfront* employs both pigeons and crosses as motifs.

Once a pattern has been established in a film, any **variation** can be significant. Marion Crane's wardrobe change in *Psycho* is an example of repetition and variation combining to produce meaning. Marion appears in a cheap hotel room with her lover Sam in the film's opening scene wearing a white bra and slip **(3.45)**. She tells Sam that she will no longer sleep with him unless he marries her. The white lingerie represents her aspirations to purity, respectability, and conventional notions of goodness. After Marion steals the $40,000 from her boss with the intention of using it to run away and start a life with Sam, she appears in her bedroom wearing an almost identical bra and slip, only this time in black **(3.46)**. The repetition of the lingerie with the variation in color suggests Marion's dual nature and underscores the fact that she has given in to her darker impulses by stealing the money.

Developing a Thesis

As we've said, a thesis statement is an opinion. However, not all opinions make for effective thesis statements. Developing a thesis is a bit of a balancing act. If your thesis is too broad, your essay will lack focus. If your thesis is too narrow, it won't be of interest to readers and you will have trouble developing it into a full-length essay.

Imagine you've viewed *Jaws* and are preparing to write an essay on the film. In looking through your screening notes, you observe that you've jotted down some ideas about how Martin Brody isn't a very admirable character in the first part of the film. You find yourself particularly critical of Brody's decision to keep the beaches open after the initial shark attack—a decision that results in the death of young Alex Kintner and, in a later attack, the death of the unidentified man in the estuary. You test your thesis by asking yourself whether someone could argue the opposite—that Brody was acting reasonably in taking into consideration the devastating economic effect that a beach closing would have on the resort community. You decide that, yes, both of these statements are opinions, and so you craft your idea into a thesis: "Martin Brody's decision to cave in to pressure from town officials to keep the beaches open after the initial shark attack is a sign of his moral weakness."

While this is a valid opinion, it has an important shortcoming as a thesis: it is too specific to serve as the basis for an entire essay. It focuses on a single plot element, and it does so in a narrow, restrictive manner. Once you've pointed out that Brody agrees to keep the beaches open against his better judgment and that this decision results in the death of the Kintner boy, your argument will have nowhere left to go. It will be difficult to generate more than a single body paragraph from such a thesis. In addition, this thesis does not shed light on the film as a whole; it ignores too many other aspects of Brody's character and it excludes too much of the story, including the entire second half of the film. If you have experienced difficulty developing sufficient ideas for a complete essay, it may have been due to the fact that your thesis was too narrow.

The solution is to expand your thesis so that it allows more room for development. Instead of concentrating solely on Brody's decision to keep the beaches open and what this decision might reveal about his moral character, we might broaden our statement regarding his shortcomings and add to our thesis that Brody overcomes these flaws in the second part of the film. We might also place Brody's story in a larger context by extrapolating a more general conclusion from his specific case: "In *Jaws* (1975), Martin Brody's story represents the dilemma of the American Everyman in the 1970s. Scared, powerless, and beset by flaws, he must somehow overcome his fears and inadequacies if he is to survive in a confusing and hostile world."

On the other hand, you must be careful not to expand your thesis so much that it becomes too general. For example, "*Jaws* is about American society" is too broad a statement to serve as an effective thesis. American society is a vast topic. What particular aspects of it are relevant to the film? What elements of the film will your essay concentrate on? You can't write effectively about every character or event in the movie. Finally, avoid vague terms such as "is about," which don't really convey anything meaningful. "*Jaws* is about American society" could simply mean that the film is set somewhere in America and has Americans in it. This would be a factual statement and would not be a valid basis for an essay.

Narrative Patterns

Films are stories and stories are about change. Most films portray a change on the part of the protagonist. Typically, this change is positive—that is, the protagonist matures or improves in some way over the course of the narrative. But in a few cases, a protagonist changes for the worse. *Taxi Driver* charts Travis Bickle's transformation from a confused and depressed loner to a psychotic killer. *The Godfather* (1972) tells the story of how Michael Corleone is corrupted by power and the desire for vengeance. When we first meet Michael, he is a model citizen, a decorated war hero who wants no part of his family's organized crime business; by the end of the film, however, he has become a cold-hearted, calculating killer, lying to his wife and sister about the fact that he has had his own brother-in-law murdered.

In other films, such as *Leaving Las Vegas* (1995) and *The Big Lebowski* (1998), the protagonists don't really change at all—or if they do, the change is so infinitesimal as to be insignificant. But even in these films, the subject of change is still at the forefront. For films in which the protagonist remains static, the subject is the inability or refusal to change. We watch with the hope or the expectation that the character will transform his life—and we may be saddened by his ultimate inability to do so, as is the case in *Leaving Las Vegas*.

We can chart a character's development with a simple diagram. The left-hand column indicates a character's qualities or traits at the beginning of the film; the right-hand column indicates the changes that take place in the character by the end of the film. For each trait and each change that you identify, you should cite one or more examples from the film. If we cite selfishness as one of Rick Blaine's character flaws at the beginning of *Casablanca*, we should cite specific examples, such as his statement, "I stick my neck out for nobody" or Captain Renault's comment that "Rick is completely neutral about everything."

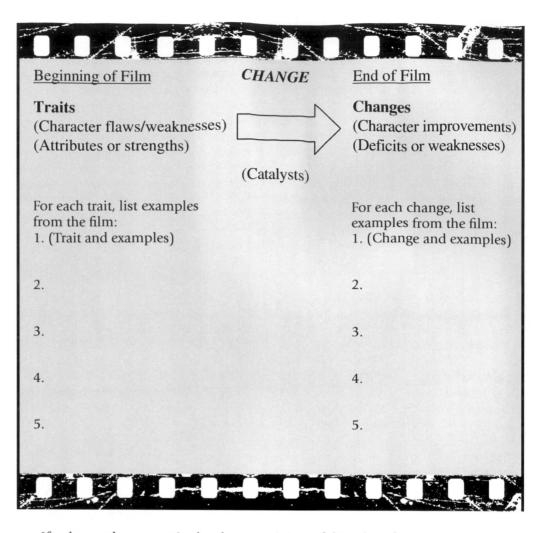

If a change does occur in the character, it is useful to identify one or more causes. The center column (Catalysts) indicates the influences that help bring about the change in the character. Try to avoid citing a specific character as a catalyst; instead, try to identify a larger force or concept as the agent of change. For example, instead of stating that the catalyst for Michael Corleone's change in character in *The Godfather* is Sollozzo, who tries to have Michael's father killed, you might say that the catalyst is violence—which intrudes on Michael's life in several forms during the course of the film, including the attempt on Don Corleone's life, the killing of Michael's brother Sonny, and the murder of Michael's wife in Sicily.

By filling in the categories shown in the diagram, we can begin to chart a character's transformation or lack of one. If we are able to identify specific character flaws in the left-hand column and corresponding improvements in the right-hand column, we may conclude that the character matures or is redeemed in the course of the film, and we can develop a thesis accordingly. In addition, by charting the protagonist's flaws and improvements and identifying specific examples of each, we are gathering supporting evidence to be used later in our argument.

Whether a character changes for the better, for the worse, or not at all is often a matter of opinion. While some viewers feel that Terry Malloy redeems himself in *On the Waterfront*, others feel that Terry doesn't really change for the better in the course of the film. They argue that his motives remain selfish throughout the story and that neither the death of Joey Doyle nor the death of "Kayo" Dugan convinces him to do the right thing; rather, his decision to testify comes only after the mob has made an attempt on his life and has killed his brother Charley; and his decision to confront Johnny Friendly in the final scene is due not to some commitment to justice and high ideals but to the fact that Friendly has taken away his livelihood and alienated him from his friends. Remember what we said about thesis statements: they are opinions, and the best way to test whether you have an opinion is to ask yourself whether one might reasonably argue the opposite. In this case, we've got two opposing views regarding the protagonist; either one may serve as the basis for an effective thesis statement.

Once you have established an opinion about the development of the protagonist's character, you may consider expanding this idea to a more general statement about the film. Ask yourself the following questions: Are there any obvious parallels between the protagonist and other characters in the film? Do those characters change in ways similar to that of the protagonist? Are there common causes for these changes? If the answer to these questions is yes, then you may be able to develop a more expansive thesis statement rather than one that addresses the development of only a single character.

Using the Character Development Diagram to Develop a Thesis

Step 1: Fill in the three categories in the diagram: Traits, Changes, and Catalysts.

Step 2: List specific examples from the film for each trait and for each change.

Step 3: Determine the dominant development trend for the character: Does she change for the better? Does she change for the worse? Is she static?

Step 4: Create a thesis statement based upon the conclusion you drew in Step 3. For example:

"Conventional wisdom states that *On the Waterfront* is the tale of Terry Malloy's redemption. On closer examination, however, it becomes clear that Terry's motives remain just as selfish at the end of the film as they were at the beginning. His character does not really change."

Or . . .

"*On the Waterfront* is a tale of redemption through violence. The protagonist, Terry Malloy, as well as secondary characters such as Dugan and Father Barry, are positively transformed through their encounters with brutality."

Charting a character's development is a simple way to identify a pattern in a specific film and develop a thesis, but you have some other slightly more advanced options available. You may, for example, compare patterns of character development in two or more films. Or you may begin with a pattern already identified by a scholar or theorist and show how a film conforms to that pattern.

In *The Hero with a Thousand Faces*, Joseph Campbell argued that myths have a common structure. Campbell studied myths from widely disparate cultures and discovered a universal pattern to the hero's adventure: "A hero ventures forth from the world of common day into a region of supernatural wonder; fabulous forces are there encountered and a decisive victory is won; the hero comes back from this mysterious adventure with the power to bestow boons on his fellow man" (30). The hero begins his adventure in a state of innocence and proceeds through a series of trials and tribulations to attain knowledge. Campbell identifies several stages in this adventure: departure, initiation, and return. Each stage contains several elements.

The departure phase of the hero's adventure consists of five elements. The first of these is **"the call to adventure."** This element of the adventure roughly corresponds to the combination of opening balance and disordering event that we discussed in Chapter 1. Some event draws the protagonist away from the mundane, familiar world and thrusts him into a realm of mystery, confusion, and danger. "The hero can go forth of his own volition to accomplish the adventure . . . or he may be carried or sent abroad by some benign or malignant agent . . . The adventure may begin as a mere blunder . . . or still again, one may be only casually strolling, when some passing phenomenon catches the wandering eye and lures one away from the frequented paths of man" (Campbell 58). In *Blue Velvet*, Jeffrey Beaumont's two disordering events (his father's stroke and the discovery of a severed ear in a vacant lot) take him into a dark and violent world very different from the mundane existence he has known both in Lumberton and away at college. "I'm seeing things that were hidden," he tells Sandy. "I'm involved in a mystery."

The second component of the departure phase is **"the refusal of the call."** If the hero refuses the call, there will be no adventure. What will follow will be merely stagnation, a story of how the hero fails to fulfill his potential. But often the reluctant hero resists the call to adventure only to accept it in the end. In *Unforgiven* (1992), William Munny initially declines the Scofield Kid's invitation to join him on his quest to collect the bounty on the two cowboys who cut up the prostitute. Rick Blaine insists on remaining neutral at the beginning of *Casablanca* ("I stick my neck out for no one," he says after Ugarte is arrested). Much of the first part of *On the Waterfront* is about Terry's reluctance to heed the call. Even comedies may incorporate "the refusal of the call": in *Bringing Up Baby*, David Huxley does his best to resist Susan Vance's attempts to draw him into the topsy-turvy adventure that will eventually transform him.

Once the call is accepted, the hero receives **"supernatural aid"** from a mentor. In *Star Wars*, Obi-Wan Kenobi guides Luke. In *The Matrix*, Neo is aided by Morpheus, who reveals to him the illusory nature of the Matrix and its possibilities. Even films that do not strictly conform to the monomyth often incorporate this story element. Terry Malloy, for example, receives spiritual guidance from Father Barry; and in *Jaws*, Martin Brody is guided on his journey into the dangerous and mysterious world of the great white shark by shark expert Matt Hooper.

Eventually the hero arrives at the edge of the known world and stands on the threshold of a zone of power and knowledge. Campbell refers to this as **"the crossing of the first threshold."** Fearsome beings stand guard over the threshold. "Beyond them is darkness, the unknown, and danger; just as beyond the parental watch is danger to the infant and beyond the protection of his society danger to the member of the tribe. The usual person is more than content, he is even proud, to remain within the indicated bounds, and popular belief gives him every reason to fear so much as the first step into the unexplored" (77–78).

The final element of the departure is **"the belly of the whale."** Having crossed the threshold, the hero enters into a realm in which he symbolically dies and is reborn. This realm is associated with contemplation, transformation, and the unconscious. "This popular motif gives emphasis to the lesson that the passage of the threshold is a form of self-annihilation" (Campbell 91). The old self must die in order for the new one to be born. In *The Matrix*, Neo dies and then, like Christ, is resurrected. In *Apocalypse Now*, Willard enters the belly of the whale when he arrives at Kurtz's nightmarish camp and is imprisoned only to emerge a changed man.

In the initiation stage, the hero undergoes a series of trials and tribulations that Campbell refers to as **"the road of trials."** The hero's ultimate task is to put aside his ego. Luke Skywalker must learn to stop thinking and give himself over to the Force. David Huxley in *Bringing Up Baby* must stop worrying about his reputation and his precious intercostal clavicle and learn to enjoy life. Other elements of the initiation include "the meeting with the goddess," "atonement with the father," and "apotheosis." In the latter, the hero finally transcends his ego and attains enlightenment through suffering and struggle.

In the final stage of the adventure, the hero returns to the world and to the community of men in order to renew or rebuild that community. Think of Willard's return upriver after he has killed Kurtz or Terry Malloy's return to the docks after he has testified against Johnny Friendly.

Campbell's monomyth is only one possible framework for analyzing narratives— and, of course, not every film corresponds to Campbell's mythological paradigm. If you do think that a film corresponds to Campbell's paradigm, such a comparison is likely to make for an interesting essay topic. It's not necessary for the film to contain every single element of the monomyth—in fact, few myths actually do contain all the elements. Your job is to identify enough elements in the film to make your argument compelling.

Ideology

Ideology is another factor to consider when developing a thesis. An ideology is a set of values, beliefs, or assumptions about the world. The concept rose to prominence in film studies after the appearance in 1970 of an influential essay by French philosopher Louis Althusser. In "Ideology and Ideological State Apparatuses (Notes Toward an Investigation)," Althusser defined ideology as "the imaginary relationship of individuals to their real conditions of existence" (162). What does this mean, and what is its significance for cinema?

In order to get a basic grasp of ideology as a concept, let's look at a series of actual historical events—the attacks of 9/11 and their aftermath—and some of the ways in which people viewed those events. The hijacking and crashing of the planes, the destruction of the towers, the American military response that followed, and the material effect that response had on the lives of people in various parts of the world (i.e., America, Afghanistan, and Iraq)—these are "real conditions of existence." But different individuals formulated different imaginary responses to these events. Many people, both in America and around the world, viewed the attacks as acts of cowardice and evil. But others, even some in America, saw the attacks as justified and heroic—a blow struck against a tyrannical superpower. Here we can see conflicting ideologies forming around the same "real conditions of existence." On the one hand, we have an ideology that imagines America is the moral compass of the world, a paragon of freedom and justice. On the other hand, we have an ideology, espoused particularly by those whose lives have been adversely impacted by American policies and actions, which views America as hypocritical at best, and as "the Great Satan" at worst. Susan Sontag, writing in *The New Yorker* just days after 9/11, drew attention to the ideological nature of the public discourse in America at the time, and in the process revealed her own ideological position:

> The disconnect between last Tuesday's monstrous dose of reality and the self-righteous drivel and outright deceptions being peddled by public figures and TV commentators is startling, depressing. . . . Where is the acknowledgement that this was not a "cowardly" attack on "civilization" or "liberty" or "humanity" or "the free world" but an attack on the world's self-proclaimed superpower, undertaken as a consequence of specific American alliances and actions?

In the 1970s, film theorists concluded that "the cinema . . . is a dense system of meaning, one that borrows from so many different discourses—of fashion, of narrative, of politics, of advertising, and so on—that it offers particularly rich possibilities for ideological understanding. . . .that the cinema is not just the product of a particular culture, but rather a projection of its most fundamental needs, desires, and beliefs" (Mayne 20–21). These theorists concentrated their attention on classical Hollywood cinema because it reflected the ideology of the dominant culture, which was white, patriarchal, industrialized, heterosexual, and capitalist. According to this view, cinema is a sort of propaganda apparatus, instilling in viewers the values of the mainstream culture—it "works to acculturate individuals to structures of fantasy, desire, dreams, and pleasure that are fully of a piece with dominant ideology" (Mayne 18).

According to this view of cinema, *It Happened One Night,* a seemingly frivolous romantic comedy, did more than simply entertain viewers when it appeared in 1934; it articulated certain fears and aspirations on the part of the culture at large—namely American women's increasing desire for sexual and economic independence, the anxieties and fears of men regarding unrestrained female sexuality, tensions between the wealthy and the working classes, and the diminished capacity of many men to provide for their families during a time of severe economic crisis (the Great Depression). But the film also did something else: it shaped its viewers into ideological subjects, causing them to identify with the stars on the screen and encouraging them in subtle ways to internalize the values expressed in the movie. Thus the film warned female viewers at the time who might, like Ellie Daniels, aspire to greater independence that those aspirations made them appear to men to be spoiled, arrogant, and cold. The film also sent the message that female independence might be all well and good (after all, a young woman needs to detach herself from her father at some point), but that ultimately every woman needs a man—ideally one who is essentially a younger, more handsome version of her father. Peter doles out an allowance to Ellie, feeds and clothes her, and at one point even spanks her. By combining romantic traits with paternal attributes, he represents a fusion of lover and father—an ideal that the film presents as highly desirable. In showing how Ellie, a rebellious young heiress, is tamed and controlled by Peter Warne, a gruff working-class reporter who has some growing up to do himself, the film conveyed to audiences that both the gap between the genders and the gap between the social classes in America could be bridged if each side gave a little.

By contrast, *Sleeping with the Enemy* (1991) addresses some of the same issues (gender, class) from a different ideological perspective. Here patriarchal authority—represented by Laura's physically abusive husband, Martin—is portrayed not as charming but malevolent, and rather than espousing class reconciliation, the film implies a correlation between evil and the Wall Street capitalist elite while associating goodness with small-town, middle-class values.

Some films are overtly ideological. D. W. Griffith's *Birth of a Nation* (1915), for example, does little to disguise its racist ideology. *Schindler's List* (1993) has a clear and obvious message about moral choice and the importance of individual courage and responsibility, and *On the Waterfront* is fairly explicit in its expression of Christian ideology (both Father Barry and Edie speak openly about Christian values). However, many other films present themselves as entertainment first and foremost. The ideological content of such films lies beneath the surface and often requires some excavation. The violence and intrigue of gangster films such as *The Godfather* and the Hawks and De Palma versions of *Scarface,* for instance, disguise the fact that these films are commentaries on American capitalism.

Film theorists often concern themselves not only with the ideology of a particular film, but with the means by which cinema turns viewers into ideological subjects—or to put it in simpler terms, the ways in which films lure viewers into adopting the dominant ideology. As Judith Mayne writes, "in order to understand how cinema functioned ideologically, it was not enough to submit films to a test to determine a political content distilled and rendered from the vehicle of the film. Rather, it was the 'vehicle' itself—the situation of film viewing, the nature of film language—that required explanation" (14). According to this view, cinema disseminates its ideological biases through the very process by which film portrays reality. As Leo Braudy and Marshall Cohen write, "One assumption of the prevailing ideological system is that cinema 'reproduces' reality but, in fact, it only reproduces the world of the dominant ideology" (660). In other words, films reinforce a view of the world that conforms to the values of the dominant culture by appearing to present the world as it really is, when in fact films shape reality to suit the dominant ideology. Let's take a very simple example: for decades Hollywood cinema portrayed a world in which people of color did not exist or existed only as minor stereotyped characters at the very margins of a story. This isn't reality so much as a social and political bias expressed on film and presented as if it were factual or true. The same may be said for classical cinema's "beauty" bias. Current mainstream cinema portrays a world in which nearly every male character looks as if he has a personal trainer on call twenty-four hours a day and nearly every female character looks like a Victoria's Secret model.

These distortions of reality are not limited to the portrayal of characters. Many of the assumptions viewers make about what constitutes a "good" or a "bad" film are based upon mainstream Hollywood film conventions. Linear narrative, "realistic" acting, the relation of sound to image, the 180-degree rule, and other elements of continuity editing such as the shot/reverse-shot combination are conceits of the classical paradigm as developed under the Hollywood studio system from the late 1920s to the 1950s. As Mayne points out, the classical paradigm still applies to films made recently. "While the history of the Hollywood studio system is the paradigm for classical cinema, the term 'classical cinema' is still often used to refer to a model of filmmaking rather than to a specific historical period, encompassing such recent films as *Fatal Attraction* or *Driving Miss Daisy*, for instance" (21).

Uncovering particular biases or ideologies in films and revealing the ways in which film form contributes to the perpetuation of these ideologies is the aim of some film theorists. Different scholars focus on different ideological aspects of cinema. Marxists scholars, for example, reveal the social and economic ideologies underlying cinema, while feminist critics examine sexual ideologies and gender biases.

Ideology and Film Theory: Two Examples

In her influential 1975 essay "Visual Pleasure and Narrative Cinema," feminist critic Laura Mulvey seeks to reveal the underlying sexist assumptions in classical cinema as well as the way in which those assumptions are imbedded in the mechanisms and techniques of the classical paradigm itself. Mulvey's essay is not an easy read. Taking Freudian psychoanalytic theory as her starting point, she argues that classical cinema presents women as the passive sexual objects of an active male gaze. In other words, men *look* while women are *looked at*. The pleasure gained by looking is referred to as **scopophilia**.

> Freud isolated scopophilia as one of the component instincts of sexuality. . . . He associated scopophilia with taking other people as objects, subjecting them to a controlling and curious gaze. His particular examples centre around the voyeuristic activities of children, their desire to see and make sure of the private and the forbidden (curiosity about other people's genitals and bodily functions, about the presence or absence of the penis and, retrospectively, about the primal scene). In this analysis scopophilia is essentially active. . . . At the extreme, it can become fixated into a perversion, producing obsessive voyeurs and Peeping Toms, whose only sexual satisfaction can come from watching, in an active controlling sense, an objectified other. (713)

"Visual Pleasure and Narrative Cinema" by Laura Mulvey, Screen, 16(3), Autumn 1975, pages 6–18. Copyright © 2009 by the John Logie Baird Centre and Oxford University Press. Reprinted by permission of Oxford University Press.

Mulvey equates scopophilia with film viewing and draws a correlation between the voyeur who receives sexual gratification from spying on his victim and the spectator who sits in a darkened theater projecting his desires onto the actors onscreen. But Mulvey also makes a second observation about cinema. She argues that film's concentration on the human form leads the spectator to identify with what he sees on the screen. The viewer recognizes the image on screen as a reflection of himself, while at the same time realizing that the onscreen image is superior to him—the image the spectator sees is "more complete, more perfect than he experiences his own body" (714). We can better understand Mulvey's point if we imagine a viewer who idealizes and aspires to be like a character in a film—say, Tyler Dirden (Brad Pitt) in *Fight Club*—but is at the same time frustrated by the fact that he cannot attain his ideal: first of all, our hypothetical viewer is not Brad Pitt, and second, life is not a movie.

Mulvey's essay is interested primarily in the implications that all this has for women. She argues that cinema designates women as passive bearers of an active male gaze. "In their traditional exhibitionist role women are simultaneously looked at and displayed, with their appearance coded for strong visual and erotic impact so that they can be said to connote *to-be-looked-at-ness*" (715). On the other hand, male characters in films are portrayed as active, controlling forces. These characters are the ones who do the looking at women and control the events of the story. In *Scarface*, for instance, Tony Camonte spends a good deal of the movie gazing with desire at Poppy and making sexually suggestive comments. The film portrays Tony rising to the top of the organized crime world in Chicago, while Poppy is often photographed in her lingerie and serves primarily as a sexual trophy in the competition between Tony and Johnny Lovo.

According to Mulvey, the film spectator merges his gaze with the gaze of the male protagonist. "As the spectator identifies with the main male protagonist, he projects his look on to that of his like, his screen surrogate, so that the power of the male protagonist as he controls events coincides with the active power of the erotic look, both giving a satisfying sense of omnipotence" (716). These tendencies are reinforced through Hollywood conventions, such as continuity editing, which perpetuate the illusion of a seamless reality and constitute, in Mulvey's words, "an ideology of representation that revolves around the perception of the subject; the camera's look is disavowed in order to create a convincing world in which the spectator's surrogate can perform with verisimilitude" (721).

The cinematic illusion, however, is under constant threat from the female image. Freud theorized that a young boy looking at the naked female body for the first time and not seeing a penis assumes that the woman has been castrated and fears that the same thing might happen to him. From that point forth, the male associates women with castration. In order to counterbalance this castration anxiety associated with women, men must either devalue women (voyeurism) or over-value them (fetishism)—Mulvey argues that classical cinema does both. Thus we often see the femme fatale devalued and punished in film noirs (Phyllis Dietrichson in *Double Indemnity*, Brigid O'Shaughnessy in *The Maltese Falcon*, Judy Barton in *Vertigo*) or we see female stars glamorized, their beauty documented by the camera—"she is no longer the bearer of guilt but a perfect product, whose body, stylized and fragmented by close-ups, is the content of the film" (719). In this way, Mulvey argues, cinema is tailored to "the neurotic needs of the male ego" (721).

Like Mulvey, Robert Ray looks at classical cinema in order to identify its ideological biases. In *A Certain Tendency of the Hollywood Cinema, 1930–1980*, Ray argues that both the formal characteristics of classical Hollywood cinema—the elements of continuity editing, the way in which style is subordinated to narrative, the illusion of seamlessness and realism—as well as its thematic conceits "serve the same ideological purpose: the concealment of the necessity for choice" (Ray 32).

Through the use of continuity editing (the 180-degree rule, the eyeline match, the match on action, the shot/reverse-shot combination, the division of space, etc.) cinema's "formal paradigm" creates an "invisible style" that conceals the myriad of choices made by the film's director and editor. Editing is an inherently fragmented process. Segments of film are divided into smaller units and combined with each other. The classical formal paradigm disguises this by creating a seamless illusion. It also conceals the necessity for choice in another way: it directs or controls what the spectator sees. "When a film narrowed the larger space of the room to the smaller units of a reverse field (say, a man and a woman exchanging glances), the audience assumed that this space, at least for the duration of the shot-reverse shots, was the only important one" (Ray 39–45).

Thematically, classic Hollywood cinema also conceals the need for choice. Ray argues that Hollywood attempts to reconcile "incompatible values." Owing to its unique history, America developed myths that conflict with each other. Ray finds the cinematic blueprint for these conflicting myths in the Western, but asserts that this thematic paradigm is at work in American films of every genre. At the heart of the paradigm is the conflict between two incompatible American tendencies represented by the official hero and the outlaw hero.

> The movies traded on one opposition in particular, American culture's traditional dichotomy of individual and community that had generated the most significant pair of competing myths: the outlaw hero and the official hero. Embodied in the adventurer, explorer, gunfighter, wanderer, and loner, the outlaw hero stood for that part of the American imagination valuing self-determination and freedom from entanglements. By contrast, the official hero, normally portrayed as a teacher, lawyer, politician, farmer, or family man, represented the American belief in collective action, and the objective legal process that superseded private notions of right and wrong. (58)

Ray's thesis is that Hollywood cinema conceals the need to choose between these incompatible tendencies in American society and attempts to preserve both sets of values. "Classic Hollywood's gallery of composite heroes (boxing musicians, rebellious aristocrats, pacifist soldiers) clearly derived from this mythology's rejection of final choices" (64).

Analysis: How to Listen and Look for Meaning

The Screening Notes Checklist below will help you focus and organize your observations about a film. Items 1–4 are designed to get you thinking about the film as a whole and to help you develop a thesis statement. Items 5–8 are intended to help you gather evidence from the film to support your thesis; these items are particularly important when you perform close readings of specific scenes.

Screening Notes Checklist

1. **Narrative Patterns:** What internal and/or external conflicts exist in the film? Is the protagonist static or dynamic? If the protagonist changes, does she change for the better or the worse? What are the catalysts for change? Does the narrative conform to the structure of Campbell's monomyth?
2. **Motifs:** What motifs occur throughout the film? What is the significance of each motif in relation to the protagonist, the antagonist, the conflict(s), or all three? How are repetition and variation used?
3. **Theme:** How does the specific conflict in the film relate to larger issues in the world? Is this specific conflict in any way symbolic? If so, what does the conflict in the film represent? What values or ideals do the protagonist and antagonist each represent?
4. **Ideology:** Does the film seem to have a particular message that it is trying to impart? Does the film send mixed messages? Does it attempt to reconcile the conflicting ideologies or philosophies it

portrays? How does it attempt to do so? Does it succeed? Does the film favor particular values or beliefs? In what ways does the film limit the world it portrays—for example, what races, classes, or genders are excluded from the story? What assumptions does the film make about the world?

5. **Sound:**
   - **Dialogue:** Are there instances in which dialogue seems to be explicitly addressing the film's themes, in which characters seem to be speaking the film's ideas? What examples are there of subtextual dialogue? What meanings are being implied and what themes are being suggested by such dialogue?
   - **Score:** How does the score contribute to the film? How is it used to highlight the film's themes?

6. **Mise-en-Scène**
   - **Setting:** What role does the setting play in relation to the plot? In what ways does the setting reflect the character and/or his circumstances? Do any elements of the setting function symbolically? Are there significant similarities or significant differences between the film's various settings?
   - **Figure position:** What patterns of proximity or distance between figures do you notice in the film? How do these patterns change over the course of the film? What do they indicate about the relationships between the characters?
   - **Costume:** What does costume reveal about a particular character? Do changes in costume correspond to changes in the character? Does costume function symbolically? How?
   - **Lighting:** What type of lighting is predominant in the film? What tone does it create? How does this relate to the characters, their situations, or both? How does the lighting function in particular scenes? For example, does a character move from light into shadow or vice versa? Does the lighting change from scene to scene in a noticeable way? What significance does this have?
   - **Framing:** Does the framing imply freedom or entrapment (is it loose or tight)? Does it imply power relationships between characters? Do certain characters tend to dominate foreground or background? Do particular characters dominate specific areas of the frame—that is, center, right, left, top, or bottom? Do these tendencies change over the course of the film? What is the effect of this?
   - **Composition:** Are certain compositional patterns prevalent? Are the compositions balanced or unbalanced? Diagonal? Circular? Does the compositional pattern change at particular points? What is the significance of this?
   - **Movement:** Are there significant movements upward or downward within the frame, particularly on the part of characters? Does this movement signify anything about the character's circumstances or psychology?
   - **Color:** Does a particular color predominate in a scene? What mood does it create? Does it have any symbolic significance? How does this relate to the circumstances of the characters?

7. **Cinematography:**
   - **Distance:** What types of shots are used? What is their effect? Are we kept at a distance with long shots, or is a sense of intimacy established with close-ups?
   - **Angle:** What camera angles are used? Do we tend to look down on particular characters or up to them? Do the angles change over the course of the film?
   - **Camera movement:** Is the camera static or mobile? Is there anything unusual about the camera movements that are used? What tone is conveyed by the camera movement—attraction, unease, revelation, chaos?

8. **Editing:** Does the film favor fewer and lengthier shots or does it use frequent cuts? How does the editing style relate to the story? Does the editing control the way in which the audience views the action, or does it allow the audience more freedom to interpret what is onscreen? Is the film edited to create physical and psychological continuity, or does the filmmaker seem to have other intentions? If the film departs from classical editing style, how does it do so and what are the effects of this?

As we mentioned earlier, one of the easiest ways to develop a thesis is to determine whether a character, usually the protagonist, does or does not change in the course of a film. You might also consider what the catalyst is for that change or, in the case of a static character, what you think prevents or inhibits a change. A more ambitious thesis might look at the character as representative of some larger group or community and interpret his ability or inability to change accordingly. For example, you might argue that Benjamin Braddock's anxiety and ambivalence about the future in *The Graduate* is representative of the attitude of a generation of privileged white American males faced with the social and political upheavals of the 1960s, including the Vietnam War, the civil rights movement, and the sexual revolution.

Another option is to identify a particular theme in a film and demonstrate how a character's development reflects that theme. If you decide, for example, that Howard Hawks's *Scarface* depicts the destructive nature of capitalism and the American dream of success, you might show how Tony Camonte's rise and fall correspond to this theme. Considerations of theme often lead to questions of a film's ideology. Try to answer the ideology questions on the checklist. What attitude does the film take towards the events it portrays? Does the film show "good" triumphing over "evil"? Or does the film seem to indicate that in the battle between good and evil the line between the two inevitably becomes blurred, as seems to be the case in both *The Departed* and *The Dark Knight*? Or does the film dispense with notions of good and evil altogether in favor of a more ambiguous approach, as is perhaps the case in *Apocalypse Now* or *Doubt* (2008)?

You might choose to focus on one or more film elements and show how they are used to create meaning or express a theme in a particular movie. An example of such an essay would be one that set out to prove the following thesis: "John Ford uses costume, setting, and lighting to express the complex relationship between the villain, the official hero, and the outlaw hero in *The Man Who Shot Liberty Valance*."

Some topics may require research. For example, you might write an essay in which you place one or more films into historical context. In the case of a paper like this, you will need to gather information on the social and political conditions in existence at the time of the film's production. How are these conditions reflected in the film? You might examine how the film reflects the production methods, techniques, and style of a particular time or genre, as in the case of film noir—or how it represents a departure from previous techniques and styles, as in the case of *Citizen Kane* with its startling use of deep focus. Another option that requires some research is to take an existing theory, ideology, or philosophy, such as Marxism or Freudian theory, and apply some of its principles to the interpretation of a film. This is, in a sense, what some feminist theorists have done by applying the theories of Freud and Lacan to particular films.

List-making

Once you have settled on a thesis statement, review your screening notes and, if necessary, the film itself. Look for specific examples to support your thesis and compile a list of these examples. If you are going to be quoting dialogue in any of your examples, this is the time to go back and make certain that you have transcribed the dialogue accurately.

Outlining

It is important that once you determine your thesis, you create an outline before you start writing your first draft. Like the grocery list we mentioned earlier in this chapter, an outline will help you focus your ideas, organize your thoughts, and work more efficiently.

A **scratch outline** will provide the most basic framework for your essay. It consists of only two elements: a thesis statement and several supporting points. Think of writing an essay as like building a stool: the thesis is the seat and the supporting points are the legs. The more legs there are on the stool, the more stable the stool will be. The more supporting points you have in your essay, the stronger your argument will be.

It's a good idea to have at least three supporting points for your thesis. This will insure that you have enough variation to develop distinct body paragraphs. It will also enable you to break down your thesis into smaller and more manageable pieces.

Let's imagine that we have developed the following thesis for a paper on *Jaws*: "*Jaws* (1975) reflects fears and concerns prevalent in American society in the mid-1970s." Just as you would eat a pizza by first cutting it into slices, you should approach your thesis statement by dividing it into smaller, more manageable components: the supporting points we mentioned above. The best method for doing this is to look at the list of examples you've compiled and try to group them into categories, identifying what the examples in each category have in common and designating them accordingly. Let's assume we have compiled the following rough list of examples to support our thesis:

- Male fear of castration (man's severed leg)

- Mrs. Kintner's concern for her son

- Corruption of public officials

- Medical examiner's dishonesty

- Brody's fear of losing his job

- Townspeople's economic concern about closing beaches

- Female sexual independence (Chrissie)

- Fear of threat from offshore

- Brody's fear for the safety of his children

- Economic fears

- Corrupt behavior of town leaders

- Post-Watergate disillusionment

- Male fears of inadequacy—Brody comparing scars

- Soviet military threat

- Class conflict (Hooper and Quint)

- Ineffectiveness of law enforcement—Brody's moral weakness regarding beach closings

- Brody's cowardice—fear of water

Our challenge is to organize the bulk of these examples into three or four categories and assign each category a designation. Some of the items on our list are more specific than others. That's not a problem at this stage. We simply want to identify examples that have a common thread and place them together in the same category. The result might look something like this.

Social Concerns

Ambivalence regarding increasing sexual independence of women

Male feelings of inadequacy

Male castration fears

Parental fears for safety of children (Kintner and Brody)

Concerns over class conflict

Political Concerns

Soviet military threat

Shark represents threat from offshore

Post-Watergate disillusionment with public officials and leaders

Corruption of mayor

Dishonesty of town medical examiner

Ineffectiveness of law enforcement

Brody's cowardice and moral inadequacy

Brody's failure to close the beaches

Brody's fear of water

Brody's physical inadequacy

Economic Concerns

Fear of overseas economic competition from Japan

Shark as embodiment of foreign threat

Fears of economic collapse

Economic fears of townspeople

Brody's fear of losing his job

A scratch outline for this essay would look like this:

Thesis: *Jaws* reflects fears and concerns prevalent in American society in the mid-1970s.

1. Social concerns

2. Political concerns

3. Economic concerns

The problem with this outline is that it is missing most of the information that is crucial to a well-developed essay. The key to a strong essay is supporting details. This means gathering specific examples from the film and organizing them into coherent paragraphs. If we were to try to convert our scratch outline into a paper without adding supporting details we would end up with a severely underdeveloped essay. The following example is a bit of an exaggeration, but it illustrates an important point: without examples you will find yourself with an essay that is too brief and does not convincingly articulate an argument.

Jaws (1975) reflects the fears and concerns prevalent in American society in the mid-1970s. Several social concerns of the time period are evident in the film. *Jaws* also expresses the political fears prevalent in America in the 1970s. Finally, many of the economic tensions and stresses being experienced by the country at the time are apparent in the film.

If your instructor has assigned you a four- or five-page paper, one paragraph (such as the one above) obviously isn't going to do the trick. Most important, a single paragraph consisting of a handful of unsupported statements isn't going to convince a reader that your point is valid. Think of yourself as an attorney, your essay as the case you're preparing, and the prospective reader as the jury. If you want a winning verdict, you're going to need to present ample evidence.

The scratch outline gives you a basic plan of development for your essay, but a **detailed outline** will make the writing process much easier. While a scratch outline consists only of a thesis and several supporting points, a detailed outline treats each supporting point as a topic sentence. A **topic sentence** is a sentence that establishes the main idea of a paragraph. A detailed outline establishes a topic sentence for each paragraph and then divides each topic sentence into several supporting points. Each supporting point is supported by specific examples from the film. The following outline template for a five-paragraph essay illustrates the various components of the essay and their relationship to each other. Paragraphs II, III, and IV are body paragraphs. This outline can be expanded to accommodate an essay of any length.

I. Introduction

    1. Title of film, year, director

    2. Brief synopsis of plot

    3. Thesis

II. Topic sentence

    1. First supporting point

        a. Example from film

        b. Example from film

    2. Second supporting point

        a. Example from film

        b. Example from film

III. Topic sentence

    1. First supporting point

        a. Example

        b. Example

    2. Second supporting point

        a. Example

        b. Example

IV. Topic sentence

    1. First supporting point

        a. Example

        b. Example

    2. Second supporting point

        a. Example

        b. Example

V. Conclusion

A detailed outline for a five-paragraph essay based upon our thesis would look like this.

I. Introduction

   1. Thesis: **Jaws** (1975) reflects the fears and concerns of American society in the mid-1970s.

II. Several social concerns of the time period are reflected in the film.

   1. Shifting gender roles

      a. Increasing sexual independence of women

         i. Chrissie luring man into deadly waters

         ii. Ellen Brody taking sexual initiative ("Want to get drunk and fool around")

      b. Male fears of inadequacy

         i. Shark as castration threat (the severed leg)

         ii. Brody's fear of water

   2. Parental concern over well-being of children in an increasingly dangerous world

      a. Mrs. Kintner's concern for son

      b. Brody's concern for sons

   3. Class conflict

      a. Hooper—wealthy and college educated

      b. Quint—working class and anti-intellectual

III. The film reflects the political concerns of America at the time.

   1. The threat posed by the shark represents the perceived threats posed to America from beyond its shores

      a. Soviet military threat

      b. Japanese economic threat

      c. Arab oil embargo threat

2. Post-Watergate disillusionment with leaders

   a. Corrupt values of mayor and Chamber of Commerce

   b. Dishonesty of the medical examiner regarding cause of Chrissie's death

3. Corruption and ineffectiveness of law enforcement and military in wake of Vietnam, civil rights movement, etc.

   a. Brody's moral weakness in keeping beaches open

   b. His cowardice embodied by fear of water

   c. His feelings of inadequacy exemplified by the scene in which Hooper and Quint compare scar stories

IV. Finally, *Jaws* reveals the economic fears and anxieties of the country during the mid-1970s.

   1. Inflation, oil shortages, and foreign competition increased American economic anxiety in the 1970s

   2. The film's events reflect these concerns

      a. The shark as an embodiment of foreign economic threats

      b. Townspeople's concerns over the economic impact of closing the beaches

      c. Brody's fear of losing his job if he doesn't go along with the mayor and the Chamber of Commerce

V. Conclusion

Writing

The three main components of an essay are the introduction, the body paragraphs, and the conclusion. In the five-paragraph essay model we used for the example outline above, the first paragraph is the introduction, the last paragraph is the conclusion, and the middle three paragraphs are the body paragraphs. Depending upon the nature of your essay, you may need to add body paragraphs or even expand your introduction to more than a single paragraph.

The purpose of the **introduction**, as its name suggests, is to introduce the thesis. The thesis should come at the end of the introductory paragraph. Placing it at the beginning is a bit like walking onstage and introducing a band *after* they have played. It defeats the purpose of the introduction. Once you state your thesis, the reader will expect you to put forth an argument supporting your opinion. If you have to backtrack and present an introduction instead, you will end up with a disorganized opening that will only confuse your reader. In many cases, students who begin their papers by immediately stating the thesis do not provide any introduction at all. This is a big mistake. An introduction contains important information about the film (or films) you are discussing and provides a critical context for your thesis. You can't write an effective paper without one.

A film paper introduction may include some or all of the following ingredients: the title, director, and production year of the film or films; the names of key characters with the names of the actors in parenthesis; a brief synopsis of the plot; background information on the film; background or context for your thesis; a transition sentence; and a thesis statement. The film's title, director, and production year are not optional; you must include them in your introduction in order for readers to know which film you're writing about. If your introduction simply mentions *Scarface*, there will be no way of knowing whether you are referring to the version directed by Howard Hawks in 1931 and starring Paul Muni or to the one directed by Brian De Palma in 1983 and starring Al Pacino. Placing the date in parentheses after the title will solve this problem.

A plot synopsis is an optional component of the introduction, but it is a good idea to include one. Be sure to keep it brief. One of the biggest mistakes students make when writing a paper for a film class is to write what amounts to an extensive plot summary rather than an analysis. You can avoid this pitfall by including the plot summary in your introduction and restricting it to no more than five or six sentences. The brief synopsis also allows you to work in another component of your introduction: the names of key characters and actors.

You don't want to simply attach your thesis to the end of your introductory paragraph. You want it to appear as if it emerges organically from discussion that precedes it. Think of your introduction as a path that will lead the reader to the thesis. Any gap in the path will trip up the reader. Your goal is to make the path as smooth as possible. You can do this by providing a transition from your general discussion of the film to the specific idea contained in your thesis. A sentence or two of background about the film will often serve as the basis for an effective transition.

Below is a sample introduction for an essay on Jean-Luc Godard's *Breathless*. The thesis appears is underlined.

Although Jean-Luc Godard's *Breathless* (1960) was not the first film of the French New Wave, it is the most iconic. Godard's film follows Michel Poiccard (Jean-Paul Belmondo), a petty thief who idolizes Humphrey Bogart, over a period of three days as he steals a car in Marseilles, shoots a policeman, and arrives in Paris where he tries to simultaneously elude the police and seduce Patricia Franchini (Jean Seberg). Michel and Patricia make love. She tells him she may be pregnant by another man, and Michel tries to convince her to run off with him to Italy. Ultimately, she betrays him to the police. Michel refuses to escape when he has the chance, and the police gun him down, shooting him in the back as he runs down the street. Patricia runs to his side. He makes a series of comical faces at her and then dies. From this rudimentary plot, Godard crafted a film that startled theatergoers with its radical innovation. <u>The striking nature of *Breathless* is due to the fact that the film is both a homage to and a repudiation of classical Hollywood filmmaking. By alluding to Hollywood genres (*film noir* in particular) Godard fosters in viewers an expectation of mainstream cinematic techniques, but the film proceeds to frustrate those expectations by employing storytelling, acting, and editing methods that create discontinuity and confusion.</u>

The final paragraph of the essay is the **conclusion**. This paragraph should briefly summarize the main points of your argument and then, in one or two sentences, explain the larger implications of your thesis.

To the very end, *Breathless* employs the strategy of presenting conventional Hollywood genre themes and situations—the femme fatale, the relentless police, the film noir hero doomed by his own romantic tendencies. But the film presents them in such a way that they resist coherent interpretation. What is the purpose, for example, of the film's intentional editing discontinuities such as the one in the final scene when Michel appears to be shot while facing the police, but is then shown bleeding from a wound to his back? Why does Michel risk his life to stay with Patricia? What are we to make of his facial expressions at the end or his final words? What motivates Patricia's actions? Why does she repeat Michel's gesture of rubbing his lips in the manner of Bogart? Ultimately, the film provides no answers to these questions. Rather, it compels viewers to question their own assumptions about movies. By subverting the conventions of classical cinema in *Breathless* and raising questions about the ways in which films construct meaning, Godard has influenced the work of a number of younger filmmakers from Martin Scorsese to Quentin Tarantino. In the process, he has left an indelible mark on film history.

The paragraphs between the introduction and the conclusion are the essay's **body paragraphs**. These paragraphs do the bulk of the heavy lifting in the essay because they articulate the argument in support of your thesis. Well-organized, articulate body paragraphs will ensure that your argument is effective. A detailed outline is half the battle when it comes to writing body paragraphs. If you have effectively outlined your paragraph, writing it is simply a matter of fleshing out the ideas, translating them into clear, grammatically correct sentences, and linking those ideas together with a few strategically placed transitions. The outline below provides a slightly more detailed body paragraph template than the one shown previously in our discussion of outlining. The number of supporting points and examples may vary depending upon the paragraph you are writing. (Note: this outline begins with paragraph II because paragraph I is the introduction, which is not shown here.)

    II. Topic sentence (the main point of your body paragraph)

        1. First supporting point (with a brief explanation if necessary)

            a. Example from film

                i. Explanation of example

            b. Example from film

                ii. Explanation of example

        2. Second supporting point

            a. Example from film

                i. Explanation of example

            b. Example from film

                ii. Explanation of example

The key to a well-developed essay is supporting details. This means gathering specific examples from the film. Let's go back to *Jaws* and imagine that we have a slightly different thesis statement this time. Our new thesis is a bit simpler than the one in our earlier example; it appears at the end of the introduction below:

With Jaws (1975), Steven Spielberg virtually created the commercial Hollywood blockbuster. The film, based on Peter Benchley's best-selling novel, tells the tale of a seaside resort community terrorized by a great white shark. After his own son is almost killed by the shark, police chief Martin Brody (Roy Scheider)convinces the town to hire local shark hunter Quint (Robert Shaw). Accompanied by marine biologist Matt Hooper (Richard Dreyfuss), they set off in Quint's boat to hunt down the rogue great white. Spielberg's shark "became an instant artifact of commercial Hollywood folklore" (Sklar 426). The film, which was preceded by an unprecedented marketing blitz that included prime-time TV spots, opened on June 25, 1975, terrified beach-going summer audiences, and became the first movie to earn over $100 million. It set the standard for future summer blockbusters and influenced filmmakers in a variety of genres, including Ridley Scott, whose *Alien* (1979) owes a debt to Spielberg's film. <u>Despite its technological and commercial innovations, however, *Jaws* is a classic narrative of redemption. Martin Brody is a flawed character who, motivated by guilt and remorse, ultimately overcomes his individual shortcomings in order to triumph over his inhuman adversary.</u>

We have three supporting points, each of which can serve as a topic sentence for a body paragraph:

1. At the beginning of the film, Brody displays several shortcomings or character flaws.

2. Eventually, he is motivated to hunt down the shark by guilt and remorse over his previous actions.

3. He ultimately overcomes his shortcomings and emerges as a hero at the end of the film.

An outline of the first body paragraph might look like this:

II. Brody has several shortcomings at the beginning of the film.

   1 His persona

      a. Scheider does not fit role of typical Hollywood leading man

      b. Brody's bookish appearance and neurotic demeanor

   2. Lack of moral fiber

      a. Agrees to keep beaches open to protect his job

      b. He knows the medical examiner is lying

   3. Cowardice

      a. Fear of water

      b. Refuses to step into water to rescue people during attack

      c. Dolly zoom allusion to Hitchcock's *Vertigo*

Below is the written version of the body paragraph we just outlined. The topic sentence is indicated in bold; the three supporting points are underlined. Note how the bulk of the paragraph consists of examples that serve to support the three main statements.

Brody has to overcome several shortcomings before he emerges as a hero at the end of *Jaws*. The first of these shortcomings is superficial but nonetheless significant in a mainstream Hollywood film: Brody's physical presence. By casting Roy Scheider as Martin Brody, Spielberg gives the audience a protagonist who does not fit the Hollywood mold established by earlier films. Scheider lacks the imposing physical stature of John Wayne, the muscularity and magnetism of Marlon Brando, the cool bravado of Humphrey Bogart, or the icy menace of Clint Eastwood. Scheider's slender build, eyeglasses, and slightly nervous mannerisms give his character the air of a neurotic New York intellectual rather than that of chief of police in a seaside community populated by macho fishermen such as Quint. Brody's second shortcoming is more substantial: he lacks moral fiber. After finding Christine's remains on the beach, he suspects that she was the victim of a shark attack. Spielberg clearly establishes this with an extreme close up of Brody typing "SHARK ATTACK" under "Probable Cause of Death" on the police report. Body's immediate impulse is to close the beach in order to protect the citizens, and yet he allows himself to be talked out of this by the town's businessmen and politicians, who worry purely about the economic impact of a beach closing. "Amity is a summer town," the mayor tells him. "We need summer dollars." Brody allows himself to be swayed by the dubious explanation that Christine was struck by a boat propeller. By setting this scene on a small two-car ferry drifting between two shores, Spielberg effectively uses mise-en-scène to reinforce the idea that Brody is both backed into a corner and morally adrift. Brody stands with his back to the ferry rail, hands braced tensely on the railing, as he is confronted by the town's leaders. He ends up backing down from his convictions and agreeing to keep the beaches open. <u>The police chief's final shortcoming is perhaps the most damning one of all for the hero of an action film: a lack of courage.</u> Not only is Brody afraid to stand up to the town's leaders, we learn that he is actually afraid of water. "We know all about you, Chief," Harry tells Brody. "You don't go in the water at all, do you?" And Brody's wife tells Hooper:"Martin hates boats. Martin hates water. Martin sits in his car when we go on the ferry to the mainland." When the Kintner boy is attacked by the shark, Spielberg,in a clear allusion to Hitchcock's *Vertigo* (1958), uses a dolly zoom shot of Brody frozen in his beach chair. This shot establishes Brody as a paralyzed protagonist in the tradition of Hitchcock's Scottie. Like Scottie, Brody fails or is unable to act at critical moments due to a paralyzing fear. After the attack, Brody rushes to the water's edge, but his hydrophobia prevents him from stepping into the water to assist the panicked bathers just as Scottie's vertigo prevents him from following Madeleine to the top of the tower. In both cases, fear incapacitates the would-be hero.

Revising

Writing is a process. Don't expect your first draft to be perfect. Once you've written a first draft, reread it carefully. Check for the following:

1. **Thesis:** Do you have a coherent thesis? Have you stated an opinion?
2. **Introduction:** Does your introduction contain all the necessary elements?
3. **Organization:** Is your essay clearly organized? Do you have at least three supporting points? Are these points distinct from each other or do some of them sound like the same point being repeated?
4. **Support:** Does your essay contain adequate support? Do you have specific examples from the film to support each of your points? Do you adequately describe and explain your examples?
5. **Focus:** Is your essay focused? Do you stick to your thesis or wander off topic? Do your paragraphs stick to the point stated in your topic sentence or do you include examples that belong in a different paragraph?
6. **Conclusion:** Did you summarize your points?
7. **Grammar, spelling, and punctuation:** Did you check for run-on sentences, fragments, subject-verb agreement, and spelling?
8. **Citing sources:** Did you follow proper MLA formatting when citing your sources?

Works Cited

Althusser, Louis. *Lenin and Philosophy and Other Essays*. Trans. Ben Brewster. New York: Monthly Review Press, 1971.

Braudy, Leo and Marshall Cohen, eds. *Film Theory and Criticism*. 7th ed. New York: Oxford UP, 2009.

Campbell, Joseph. *The Hero with a Thousand Faces*. Princeton: Princeton UP, 1949.

Ebert, Robert. "Movie Review: Blue Velvet." *Chicago Sun Times*. 19 Sept. 1986. Rogerebert.com. Web. 9 Aug. 2010.

Mayne, Judith. *Cinema and Spectatorship*. New York: Routledge, 1993.

Mulvey, Laura. "Visual Pleasure and Narrative Cinema." *Film Theory and Criticism*. 7th ed. Ed. Leo Brady and Marshall Cohen. New York: Oxford UP, 2009. 711–22.

Ray, Robert. *A Certain Tendency of the Hollywood Cinema, 1930-1980*. Princeton: Princeton UP, 1985.

Sklar, Robert. *Film: An International History of the Medium*. 2nd ed. New York: Prentice-Hall, 2002.

Sontag, Susan. "Tuesday, and After." *The New Yorker*. 24 Sept. 2001. LexisNexis. Web. 5 Aug. 2010.

CHAPTER 7

Close-Up: On the Waterfront (1956)

7.1

Background

Elia Kazan's *On the Waterfront* falls into a category of films sometimes referred to as "problem pictures." The term refers not to problems with the films themselves, but rather to the fact that these films—*I Am a Fugitive from a Chain Gang* (1932), *Black*

Fury (1935), *Dead End* (1937), *The Grapes of Wrath* (1940), *Pinky* (1949), *The Wild One* (1953), *Rebel Without a Cause* (1955), and *Imitation of Life* (1959), to name a few—tackled social problems such as poverty, corruption, racism, teen rebellion, and the difficulty of returning veterans adjusting to civilian life. Social problem pictures, elements of which can be found even in early gangster films such as *Scarface*, reached their heyday in the late 1940s, when films such as *The Best Years of Our Lives* (1946) and *Gentlemen's Agreement* (1947) met with great commercial and critical success.

The appeal to Kazan of material that cast a critical gaze upon social and political aspects of American life may have been due in part to his perception of himself as an outsider. Born to Greek parents in Istanbul, Turkey, in 1909, he came to New York City in 1913. Shy, socially awkward, and stifled by a father who disapproved of his artistic aspirations, he grew up keenly aware of his own otherness: "I was a secretive freak, full of unexpressed longings, unrevealed crushes, jealousies equally unexercised, fears of intangibles, hopes crushed" (Kazan 28). Describing his experience among the "Anglos" at Williams College, he wrote in his autobiography: "Not accepted, I made it clear that I didn't want to be accepted. I was outside and I liked it" (48).

After Williams, Kazan attended Yale Drama School and upon graduation returned to New York City, where in 1932 he joined the Group Theatre directed by Lee Strasberg and Howard Clurman. The Group declared theater a "collective art" and strove to bring about a revolution in the medium. Its primary weapon in this struggle was the Method, an acting technique pioneered by Russian director Konstantin Stanislavski, adapted by Strasberg, and put into practice most famously by actors such as Marlon Brando and James Dean. As Kazan described it, "The essential and rather simple technique . . . consists of recalling the circumstances, physical and personal, surrounding an intensely emotional experience in the actor's past. It is the same as when we accidentally hear a tune we may have heard at a stormy or an ecstatic moment in our lives, and find, to our surprise, that we are re-experiencing the emotion we felt then, feeling ecstasy again or rage and the impulse to kill" (63). During this time, Kazan became involved with the leftist Theater of Action and joined the Communist Party for a short time.

Informed by his sense of alienation as both an artist and an immigrant, and influenced by his experience with the Group, his brief flirtation with Communism, and a 1934 tour through the working-class underside of the segregated American South, Kazan found himself drawn to gritty realist narratives that addressed socially and politically volatile issues from a liberal perspective. As Richard Schickel has observed of *Death of a Salesman*, which Kazan directed on Broadway in 1949 to great critical acclaim, "Underneath its rough poetic diction we are obliged to recognize that this is a very political play—a critique of American consumer capitalism and what it costs those who, like Willy, mindlessly serve it" (188). In 1947, Kazan directed *Gentleman's Agreement*, an indictment of anti-Semitism in America made at a time when Jews were not even mentioned in films. The subject matter was considered so volatile that Jewish studio heads, afraid of attracting attention and stirring up controversy, urged producer Darryl Zanuck to drop the project. Zanuck (who was a Protestant) refused. The film went on to win an Academy Award for Best Picture and garnered Kazan an Oscar for Best Director.

Kazan's liberal politics and penchant for controversial material placed him in conflict with Joseph Breen's Production Code Administration (PCA) throughout his career. In his efforts to bring *A Streetcar Named Desire* (1951) to the screen, Kazan battled with Breen, Martin Quigley, and the Catholic Church's Legion of Decency over close-ups of Stella that were deemed too erotically charged and seemingly benign lines of dialogue that the censors felt hinted too strongly at Stanley's rape of Blanche, references to which were forbidden under the Production Code. As late as 1960, Kazan found himself clashing with the PCA and the Legion of Decency over the candid sexual content of *Splendor in the Grass*.

There are clear parallels between *On the Waterfront*, the tale of a washed-up prizefighter-turned-street-thug who decides to inform on his mob associates, and events in Kazan's own life. In 1932, Kazan joined the Communist Party. He resigned nineteen months later after a disagreement over the party's attempts to control the Group Theatre. In January 1952, Kazan was called to appear before the House Committee on Un-American Activities (HUAC), the congressional standing committee dedicated to investigating suspected Communists.

HUAC targeted current and former Communists in the film industry in large part because of the power and influence that Hollywood wielded over public opinion. There was fear on the part of many on the political right that the studios would disseminate "Red" propaganda disguised as entertainment. The Motion Picture Association of America, eager to portray the industry as patriotic and to protect its profits, vowed: "We will not knowingly employ a Communist or a member of any party or group which advocates the overthrow of the government of the United States by force or by any illegal or unconstitutional methods." Eventually the Hollywood blacklist swelled to several hundred names, including notables such as Charlie Chaplin, Orson Welles, and Paul Robeson.

At his first appearance before HUAC, Kazan testified about his own nineteen-month stint in the Communist Party but declined to name others. Unsatisfied, the committee subpoenaed him a second time. When Kazan reappeared in April of that year, he named sixteen individuals who had at one time been associated with the party. A number of Kazan's friends and colleagues felt betrayed by his testimony. Brando vowed never to work with him again but went back on his word to make *On the Waterfront*, in which he plays a character who follows the dictates of his conscience by naming names to the Waterfront Crime Commission and as a result finds himself reviled by former friends and enemies alike.

Analyzing the Film

Character Development

As we said in Chapter 6, films are stories and stories are about change. Most films portray a change on the part of the protagonist. Typically, this change is positive—that is, the protagonist matures or improves in some way over the course of the narrative. We can chart a character's development with a simple diagram, in this case one that tracks the character's change for the better:

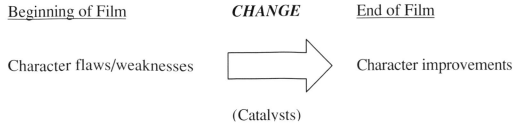

In *The Hero with a Thousand Faces*, Joseph Campbell argues that myths have a common structure. The hero begins in a state of innocence and proceeds through a series of trials and tribulations to attain knowledge. Films are cultural myths, and so it is no accident that they often employ the structure described by Campbell. Let's take *Star Wars* (1977) as an example. When we first meet Luke Skywalker, he is immature and impetuous. During the course of the film, he gains knowledge and mastery of the Force, becomes a true Jedi, and thus fulfills his heroic destiny. The hero's journey from innocence to knowledge entails great sacrifice. Luke suffers the loss of his aunt and uncle as well as the loss of his mentor, Obi-Wan Kenobi. In addition, during the film's climax, most of the rebel fighter force is destroyed and Luke himself nearly perishes.

You'll note that in the above diagram, change is brought about by means of one or more catalysts. A catalyst is an agent that provokes change. Often there is more than one catalyst at work in a film. In *Stars Wars*, one of the catalysts is violence. Luke may have been destined to become a Jedi no matter what, but violence certainly accelerates his transformation from an innocent boy into a mature hero. He initially refuses the call to action, declining to accompany Obi-Wan on his quest to rescue Princess Leia, and finally agrees to do so only after he discovers that Imperial storm troopers have murdered his aunt and uncle and destroyed his home. In addition, he learns to put aside his ego and give himself over to the Force only after witnessing the self-sacrifice of Obi-Wan during his battle with Darth Vader. Significantly, it is the voice of his dead mentor that guides Luke in the film's climactic scene. Luke's progression to each new stage of the hero's journey is fueled by violence and loss.

A character's progression from a flawed condition or a state of "sin" to an improved state may be characterized as redemption. Redemption has religious connotations, so literary and cinematic works sometimes employ religious imagery and allusions in order to underscore the redemption theme. The concept plays a particularly important role in Christian doctrine. In *The Matrix* (1999), the parallels between Neo's redemption of mankind and the story of Christ are emphasized by allusions to the Gospel and to Christian theology: Trinity's name references the Holy Trinity, and Neo's death and resurrection recall the crucifixion and resurrection of Christ.

Character development is often a good place to begin when analyzing a film. Kazan's own notes for *On the Waterfront* indicate that the transformation of Terry Malloy was the focus of the film for him. "Theme," he wrote," The Motion Picture is about one thing only: a Young man who has let his dignity slip away, regains it!" In a 1953 letter to Brando, he stated the theme even more succinctly: "A Bum becomes a man" (Neve 83).

We can chart Terry's development from a "bum" to a "man" by using our change diagram. In the "Beginning of Film" column on the diagram below, list five character flaws displayed by Terry Malloy in the first part of the film. For each flaw, list one specific example from the film that illustrates the flaw. In the "End of Film" column, list an example from the film that demonstrates Terry has overcome this flaw. Under "Catalysts," identify two factors that accelerate Terry's transformation. These catalysts should not be individual characters. It is far more productive to identify a force or a concept as a catalyst as we did in our *Star Wars* example. In other words, you should not list Edie as a catalyst even though she is one. Rather, see if you can identify what force or concept Edie represents and list that as a catalyst.

Let's assume you identified selfishness as one of the character flaws Terry displays in the beginning of the film. The next step is to identify examples from the film that you can cite to support this. You might point out that in his narrow-minded focus on his own comfort, safety, and well-being to the exclusion of all else, Terry causes harm to other members of the community. In order to stay in the good graces of Johnny Friendly, he facilitates Joey Doyle's murder. Afraid that the mob will kill him if he rats and that Edie will reject him if she finds out that he played a role in the murder, Terry then prolongs Edie's emotional suffering by withholding from her information that would enable her to put closure on her brother's death. Terry's selfishness and cowardice are consistently contrasted with Edie's fearlessness and lack of regard for her own safety. While she risks her life to search for Joey's killer, a frightened Terry hides the truth from her and advises her to adopt his own self-centered philosophy. "You better go back to that school out

Beginning of Film	CHANGE	End of Film
Character flaws/weaknesses		Character improvements
	(Catalysts) List *two* catalysts 1. 2.	
1. Flaw and example		1. Example of flaw overcome
2. Flaw and example		2. Example of flaw overcome
3. Flaw and example		3. Example of flaw overcome
4. Flaw and example		4. Example of flaw overcome
5. Flaw and example		5. Example of flaw overcome

in Daisyland," he tells her. "You're driving yourself nuts, you're driving me nuts. Quit worrying about the truth all the time. Worry about yourself."

Terry's selfishness and cowardice are once again on display in a conversation with Father Barry in which the priest urges him to testify before the Crime Commission (urges confession—religious symbol).

TERRY: If I spill my life ain't worth a nickel.
FATHER BARRY: And how much is your soul worth if you don't?

Here the dialogue explicitly refers to the theme of redemption. By changing—by exchanging selfishness for selflessness—Terry can not only defeat Johnny Friendly and the mob, he can also redeem his soul, which is ultimately what he does.

This raises the question of causality. What is the catalyst for Terry's transformation? Edie's love, certainly, but also the deaths of Joey, Dugan, and Charley. Love and death—or Eros and Thanatos, as the ancient Greeks would have put it.

We may then formulate a thesis: "In *On the Waterfront*, Terry Malloy is a deeply flawed character who is redeemed in the end through the twin forces of Eros (love) and Thanatos (death)." We would want to devote at least one body paragraph to establishing Terry's flaws, citing examples from the film. We might then devote one paragraph to the effect of Edie's love on Terry and another paragraph to the cumulative effects on Terry of Joey's, Dugan's, and Charley's deaths. How does each death move Terry closer to redemption? Finally, we might spend one body paragraph demonstrating Terry's transformation at the end of the film into a mature man, a character who "stands up for what he knows is right."

In addition to the protagonist, secondary characters in a film may change as well. This is certainly the case in *On the Waterfront*. (In fact, the novel that Budd Schulberg later wrote, based upon his screenplay for the film, made Father Barry's transformation the focus of the story and relegated Terry's struggle to the status of catalyst.) We can apply our change diagram to a number of secondary characters in the film with meaningful results. We might then devote an entire paper to the thesis that Terry's transformation is only one among many in the film. Edie, Father Barry, Dugan, and Charley also change.

It is important to note that changes in character are not always for the better. Complex characters often transform in a number of ways, only some of which are positive or desirable. A character may gain valuable knowledge and experience of life, while in the same time losing his innocence and optimism. In *Blue Velvet*, for example, Jeffrey Beaumont's investigations reveal to him deep truths about himself and about his picture-perfect American community; in the process, he discovers his own potential for evil.

 PAUSE TO CONSIDER:

Chart the complex changes in either Edie Doyle or Father Barry. In what ways does the character change for the better? In what ways does he or she change for the worse? In your opinion, do the changes for the better ultimately outweigh the changes for the worse? In other words, is what has been lost worth what has been gained? Why or why not?

Dialogue

Dialogue can reveal character psychology, signal change in a character, or express thematic content. It can do this either explicitly or implicitly.

When Terry tells his brother, "I could have been a contender . . . I could have been somebody . . . instead of a bum, which is what I am," he is clearly referring to his lost potential, disappointment, and self-loathing. We don't have to read between the lines to grasp his meaning. And when he tells Charley, "It was you," it is clear that he is blaming his brother for what has become of him. This is an instance of character psychology being revealed through explicit dialogue. It is also an instance of dialogue signaling a change in the character. Up to this point in the film, Terry has lacked the courage to speak up about things that he knows are wrong. He is disturbed by Joey Doyle's murder, but his protests to Johnny Friendly never amount to much more than a sheepish complaint: "I just figured I should have been told." He has been silently harboring resentment over the fact that Charley robbed him of his shot at a title fight. Despite this, he will not admit out loud that his own brother sold him out to fix a bet until the scene in the taxi. In an earlier scene up on the roof with Glover, the Crime Commission investigator, Terry almost blurts out the truth, but catches himself.

TERRY: If I'd have put him down, I'd have had a title shot. I was ready that night.
GLOVER: You sure looked it. That's when I figured it was all over.
TERRY: It was all over, except for the lousy bet! My own—
GLOVER: Yeah?

Terry's aborted revelation to Glover sets up the exchange with Charley in the cab, two scenes later. The repetition of the reference to Terry's lost shot at the title fight alerts us to the fact that something important is about to be revealed in the taxi scene. The variation (this time, Terry speaks the truth instead of keeping silent) signals us that a significant change has occurred in Terry's character. It also foreshadows subsequent scenes in which he speaks the truth, first to the Crime Commission and then later to Johnny Friendly's face.

The difference between explicit and implicit, or between text and subtext, can best be illustrated by the following two excerpts of dialogue from the film. The first excerpt is from Terry's dialogue at the beginning of the scene in the bar with Edie.

TERRY: Then they stuck Charley and me in a dump they call a "children's
             home." Boy, that was some home. Anyhow, I ran away from there and
             fought in the club smokers and peddled papers and Johnny Friendly
             bought a piece of me.

The second excerpt is from Edie's dialogue in the next scene. Glover and his partner have just served Terry with a subpoena, which he tears up. Edie realizes that Terry knows much more than he has been letting on, and she becomes angry that he won't tell her who killed Joey.

EDIE: Pop said Johnny Friendly used to own you. I think he still owns you.

In the first excerpt, the text (or the explicit meaning) of Terry's dialogue is that Johnny Friendly invested in him financially as a fighter. But the dialogue also has an ironic, implied meaning, which is that Terry is not his own man, that Johnny Friendly controls him, that Friendly has in fact bought Terry's loyalty and his silence. Edie's dialogue makes this implicit meaning explicit. The fact that she does so indicates the level of her anger at Terry. She is no longer trying to spare his feelings by hiding the truth.

In the above examples, dialogue reveals the thoughts and feelings of characters. Dialogue can also be used to express the film's themes. Much of Father Barry's dialogue, for example, serves as an explicit statement of the film's religious theme. In the eulogy he delivers in the ship's hold following Dugan's death, the priest draws a clear connection between events in the film and events in the Gospel: "Some people think the Crucifixion only took place on Calvary. They better wise up. Taking Joey Doyle's life to stop him from testifying is a crucifixion. Dropping a sling on Kayo Dugan because he was ready to spill his guts tomorrow . . . that's a crucifixion. Every time the mob puts the crusher on a good man, tries to stop him from doing his duty as a citizen, it's a crucifixion. And anybody who sits around and lets it happen, keeps silent about something he knows has happened, shares the guilt of it just as much as the Roman soldier who pierced the flesh of Our Lord to see if He was dead." Father Barry's explicit Christian dialogue draws our attention to the implicit (or subtextual) meaning of certain events in the film: specifically the symbolic nature of the sacrifices made by Joey Doyle and "Kayo" Dugan, and of the sacrifice that will be made later by Terry. (Explicitly or textually, Joey Doyle is murdered because he plans to testify against the mob. Implicitly or subtextually, he sacrifices himself for his fellow man; he is crucified so that Terry and the longshoremen may be redeemed.) In this case, the priest's dialogue serves as a sort of commentary on the film's plot, interpreting the meaning of important events in the story for the benefit of viewers who might not have grasped their symbolic significance.

Mise-en-Scène and Cinematography

On the Waterfront presents something of a contradiction in terms of both its mise-en-scène and its cinematography. The film blends realism with formalism in the same way that Brando's acting, as Brian Neve has observed, "is both naturalistic and baroque" (86), realistic and highly stylized. The film was influenced by Italian Neorealism, and many scenes have the stark feel of documentary footage: back alleys and seedy bars, longshoremen gathering for the shapeup, tenement rooftops crowded with television antennas and pigeon coops. In addition, Kazan employs the Neorealist strategy of casting nonprofessionals alongside professional actors. But unlike quintessential Neorealists such as Roberto Rossellini, who de-dramatized key narrative moments such as the killing of the pregnant Pina in *Rome Open City* and claimed, "If I mistakenly make a beautiful shot, I cut it out" (Cousins 192), Kazan created carefully composed shots that highlighted the intense emotions of his characters and made conspicuous use of visual symbolism. In 7.2, for example, Edie's expression reveals her growing curiosity about Terry, while her benevolent influence over him is underscored by the presence beside her of a television antenna resembling a crucifix.

PAUSE TO CONSIDER:

Keeping in mind our earlier discussion of Father Barry's dialogue in relation to Joey Doyle's death, consider the shot of Joey Doyle's corpse (**7.3**). How are elements of mise-en-scène (in this case, figure position and props) used to create meaning? Why do you think Kazan chose to have the policeman cover Joey's body with newspaper instead a sheet? How does the choice of prop (the newspaper) add to the meaning of the scene?

Kazan's mise-en-scène makes use of a number of visual motifs such as pigeons and crosses of various types. Fences also serve as an important visual motif in the film. They appear in several forms and function in a variety of ways. First, they contribute to the overall atmosphere of the film and the environment in which the characters live. When we think of fences, we think of enclosure and imprisonment. This suits the story because so many of the characters, including Terry himself, are trapped by circumstances, imprisoned by their poverty and powerlessness. Terry is like a caged animal: physically powerful, even dangerous, but penned in by the mob, domesticated, his spirit broken and all the fight taken out of him. Kazan emphasizes

7.2
The cross motif makes its appearance in the form of a rooftop television antenna.

this view of Terry by repeatedly presenting him caged inside a pigeon coop (7.4), which also associates him with the qualities that the pigeons represent: innocence, vulnerability, and fidelity.

The honest longshoremen in the film are also fenced in by the mob, trapped in a vicious cycle of poverty. The dialogue supports this, as in the scene in which Pop Doyle is forced to borrow money at a usurious rate from J.P., the mob's loan shark.

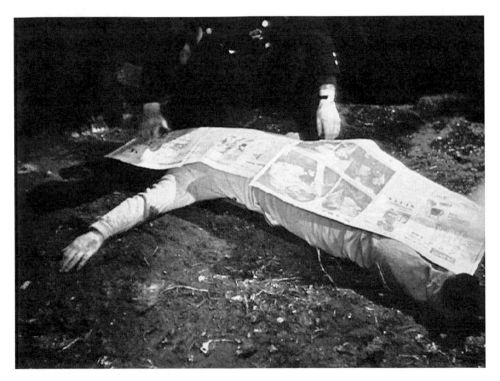

7.3
A policeman covers Joey Doyle's body with a newspaper featuring wedding photos of Marilyn Monroe and Joe DiMaggio.

7.4
Terry caged.

7.5
Another example of the film's fence motif.

When J.P. informs Pop that he is three weeks behind on his payments but that he is willing to take a chance on him anyway, Dugan replies, "Some chance at ten percent a week, and if we don't borrow, we don't work."

The spiked fence that is ubiquitous in the film also underscores the violence of the waterfront environment. In **7.5**, the fence spikes directed at Terry's throat foreshadow the threat on his life that will come later in the film, but they also foreshadow the imminent death of Joey Doyle.

In addition to contributing to the overall atmosphere of the film, the fence motif is employed by Kazan to influence the audience's feelings toward Terry. In **7.5**, the fence, in combination with the high camera angle, distances the audience from Terry and diminishes our sympathy for him. His criminal status is underscored by positioning him behind the bars of the fence. He is set apart, physically separated from the audience by the spiked posts traversing the frame. In addition, his stature is diminished by the camera angle. We literally "look down" on Terry as he does Johnny Friendly's bidding, while in the low-angle reverse shot we look *up* at the window to Joey Doyle, who is about to be murdered for standing up to the mob.

Once again, it is helpful to look for patterns of repetition and variation. A change in mise-en-scène from one scene to another can signal changes in a character. As Terry transforms from "a bum" into a hero, the high-angle shots used to diminish him earlier in the film give way to low-angle shots (**7.6**) that make him appear more imposing and emphasize his moral and ethical supremacy over Friendly and the mob. When high-angle shots appear late in the film, they are used to diminish the stature of Johnny Friendly and his thugs, as in **7.7**. Note how Terry occupies both the foreground and the high ground in this shot, while Johnny Friendly is positioned low and in the background.

Kazan also changes figure position to illustrate this shift in Terry's character. Note the consistent shot composition of **7.8** and **7.9**, with Terry occupying the lower right-hand corner of the frame and the other characters placed above him on the left. The eyelines all flow from the upper left to the lower right, emphasizing Terry's subordinate status, his powerlessness, and his moral weakness.

In one of the earliest scenes in the film, the figure position implies Johnny Friendly's restraint of Terry (**7.10**). The mob boss physically leans on Terry, foreshadowing the way in which later in the film he will "lean on" him to keep his mouth shut to the Crime Commission and at the same time referring back to the fact that he forced Terry to throw the fight that would have given him a title

7.6
A low angle-shot elevates Terry towards the end of the film.

7.7
Terry and Johnny Friendly prepare to square off.

7.8

Eyelines diminish Terry...

7.9
...in the first part of the film.

shot. Terry's lingering bitterness about the thrown fight is reignited by Big Mac's comment: "The only arithmetic he ever learned was hearing the referee count to ten." Johnny's position implies a form of restraint, while Charley literally (or explicitly) restrains Terry from going after Big Mac (7.11). In both cases, the mise-en-scène emphasizes that Terry has been "held down" or "held back" by the two men. It is worth noting that when Terry stands up to confront Big Mac, he disrupts the pattern of composition in which he has been positioned as the lowest figure in the frame, and now, by virtue of the angle and position of the camera, he appears to rise above the other characters in the shot and dominate the central portion of the frame (7.11). The figure position established in these early scenes is reversed in the climactic scene late in the film (7.7). Now Terry occupies the high ground, towering above the mobsters, in a shot that has been foreshadowed by the aborted confrontation with Big Mac.

8.10
Figure position signals...

8.11
. . . character psychology in *On the Waterfront*.

PAUSE TO CONSIDER:

The change in Terry's character (as well as the change in the audience's perception of him) is further signaled by differences in mise-en-scène and cinematography between Joey's murder (**7.5**) and Terry's conversation with Edie later in the film (**7.1**), after he has rescued her from the church and begun to reveal a softer side of himself. Note the change in camera angle. How does this alter our perception of Terry? What effect does the change in lighting have on our perception of the character? What differences do you notice in Terry's position and body language between the two scenes? What possible meanings can you extrapolate from this?

Sound

On the Waterfront was the only film score Leonard Bernstein ever wrote. While Kazan reportedly was dissatisfied with some elements of the score that he considered overly dramatic, the music captures Terry's dual nature, and its echoes can later be heard in Bernard Hermann's score for *Taxi Driver*, another film about alienation and divided masculinity (Scorsese, who saw *On the Waterfront* when he was twelve years old, cites Kazan's film as a major influence). Bernstein's score alternates between harsh dissonance and aching lyricism. Scenes of tension and violence down on the docks are accompanied by thundering drums and blaring brass, while the Hoboken rooftops, photographed with a sort of gritty urban romanticism, provide a sense of isolation and refuge that is underscored by strings (including ethereal harp strains) and plaintive horn solos. These musical elements emphasize not just the dual nature of the city, its poverty and wealth, its misery and beauty, but also the divided nature of Terry Malloy, who contains within him the potential for both violence and grace, both sin and redemption.

Diegetic sound also plays a key role in the film. The foghorns and train whistles that punctuate the scenes are used variously to transition between scenes, call our attention to key bits of dialogue, and the emotions of the characters. The train whistle

(00:12: 06) that signals the transition between Terry's rooftop conversation with Tommy about the pigeons and the shapeup in which Terry meets Edie for the first time in the film ties the two locations together and also signals a change of tone from the lyrical and contemplative space of the rooftop to the harsh pragmatism of the docks. Terry must hide the softer side of himself that he has just revealed in his concern for and identification with the pigeons, and he must don the cold, hard mask of the thug in preparation for what awaits him on the docks. The train whistle also anticipates Big Mac's whistle, which calls the longshoremen to attention and signals the world of work, necessity, and material need. Here the train's whistle cuts through the two scenes like a knife, dividing the world of romantic fantasy (Terry's fantasy of living the carefree life of a pigeon) from the harsh reality of economic necessity. A similar meaning is conveyed by the ship's horn that drowns out Terry's voice (01:03:05) as he tries to explain to Edie his role in Joey's murder: the longings and aspirations of individuals are obliterated by the harsh mercantile exigencies of the waterfront.

Works Cited

Cousins, Mark. *The Story of Film*. New York: Thunder's Mouth Press, 2004.

Kazan, Elia. *Kazan: A Life*. New York: Knopf, 1988.

Neve, Brian. *Elia Kazan: The Cinema of an American Outsider*. London: IB Taurus, 2009.

Schickel, Richard. *Elia Kazan*. New York: HarperCollins, 2005.

Exercises

It Happened One Night (1934)

Close Reading:

Watch the film's opening scene several times; then, write a description and an analysis of the scene. The still images included in this section are intended only to aid you with your screening notes. **You should consider the entire scene, not just these shots.** Make notes in the spaces provided. Use the guidelines listed below for all close reading exercises.

Part 1: Description

Describe the scene in detail, concentrating on important shots. You must use film terminology to describe what appears onscreen. Include references to:

- Camera distances and angles
- Camera movements
- Lighting
- Shot selection and combination (editing)
- Score (music); diegetic and nondiegetic sound
- Sound effects
- Dialogue
- Figure position, gestures, facial expressions (acting)
- Movement within the frame
- Décor and other elements of setting
- Props

Part 2: Analysis

Develop a thesis in which you explain what meaning is being created by the various film elements you have just described. Analyze the way in which these elements (see above) contribute to the overall meaning of the scene. For example, what does a particular shot in combination with an actor's facial expression or eye movement tell us about the character, the situation, the film's theme, or all three? How is lighting used to convey meaning? How does the score affect the tone of the scene? You must give specific examples for each element that you discuss. Your analysis may make reference to the film as a whole but should focus on the specific scene.

_____

_____

_____

_____

_____

_____

_____

_____

_____

_____

_____

_____

_____

_____

_____

_____

_____

_____

_____
_____
_____
_____
_____
_____
_____
_____
_____
_____
_____
_____
_____
_____
_____
_____
_____
_____
_____
_____
_____
_____
_____
_____

Double Indemnity (1944)

Close Reading:

Watch Chapter 13 on the DVD ("A Troubling Hunch," 1:08:38–1:13:45); then, write a description and an analysis of the scene. The still images included in this section are intended only to aid you with your screening notes. **You should consider the entire scene, not just these shots.** Make notes in the spaces provided.

_____

_____

_____

_____

_____

_____

_____

_____

_____

_____

_____

_____

_____

_____

_____

_____

_____

_____

_____

_____

_____

_____

_____

_____

_____

_____

_____

_____

_____

_____

_____

_____

_____

_____

_____

_____

_____

On the Waterfront (1954)

Close Readings:

1. View Chapter 9 on the DVD. This is the scene in which Terry and Edie talk in the playground after he has helped her escape from the thugs who have broken up the meeting in the church. Do a close reading of the scene, paying particular attention to dialogue and elements of mise-en-scène. What role does the setting play in this scene? How does it contribute to the tone and atmosphere of the scene? How does it elucidate the characters? How are props and wardrobe used in this scene, particularly the glove that Edie drops? Are significant visual elements from earlier scenes repeated here—for example, the fence that appears toward the end of the scene? If so, what variations do you notice, and how are they significant? Analyze the figure positions of Terry and Edie. What do they tell you? How does the fog contribute to the meaning of the scene?

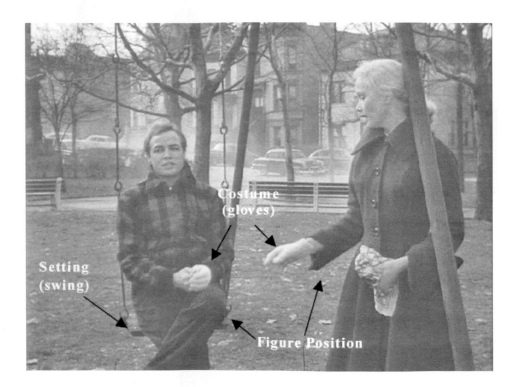

_____

_____

_____

_____

_____

_____

_____

_____

_____

_____

_____

_____

_____

_____

_____

_____

_____

_____

_____

_____

_____

_____

_____

_____

2. View Chapter 11 on the DVD ("Up on the Roof"). Write a description and detailed analysis of this scene. Consider in particular the use of dialogue, setting, figure position, camera angles, and editing.

_____

_____

_____

_____

_____

_____

_____

_____

_____

_____

_____

_____

_____

_____

_____

_____

_____

3. View Chapter 15 on the DVD ("Dropping a Sling on Dugan"). Write a description and detailed analysis of the scene. Pay particular attention to dialogue, elements in the setting, camera angles, editing, and movement within the frame. How are the first two shots shown below used to create foreshadowing in this scene?

_____

_____

_____

_____

_____

_____

_____

_____

_____

_____

_____

_____

_____

_____

_____

Compare and Contrast:

Kazan was influenced by Italian neorealism when he was shooting *On the Waterfront*, but despite this influence Kazan's film adheres to many of the principles of classical Hollywood cinema. Compare Pina's death scene from *Rome, Open City* to Charley's death scene in *On the Waterfront*. What similarities do you see in terms of mise-en-scène, editing, and narrative? What crucial differences do you see?

_____

_____

_____

_____

_____

_____

_____

_____

_____

_____

_____

_____

_____

_____

_____

_____

_____

_____

_____

_____
_____
_____
_____
_____
_____
_____
_____
_____

_____
_____
_____
_____
_____
_____
_____
_____
_____
_____
_____

_____

_____

_____

_____

_____

_____

_____

_____

_____

_____

_____

_____

_____

_____

_____

_____

Vertigo (1958)

Close Reading/Compare and Contrast:

Review the following two scenes from Alfred Hitchcock's *Vertigo*: the scene in Midge's apartment that takes up all of Chapter 3 on the DVD (from 0:05:00–0:11:19) and the scene in which Scottie first sees Madeleine at Ernie's (0:16:52–0:18:29).

Part 1: Description

Describe the scenes in detail, concentrating on important shots. You must make reference to cinematography, setting, acting, costume, editing, lighting, sound, and any other elements of the clip that seem important. You must use film terminology to describe what appears onscreen. Include references to:

- Camera distances and angles
- Camera movements
- Lighting
- Shot selection and combination (editing)
- Score (music); diegetic and nondiegetic sound
- Sound effects
- Dialogue
- Figure position, gestures, facial expressions (acting)
- Movement within the frame
- Décor and other elements of setting
- Props

Part 2: Analysis

Develop a thesis in which you explain what meaning is being created by the various film elements you have just described. Analyze the way in which these individual elements (see above) contribute to the overall meaning of each scene. What does a particular shot in combination with an actor's facial expression or eye movement tell us about the character, the situation, the film's theme, or all three? How do the two scenes relate to each other in terms of the film's meaning? Do they, for example, reveal different aspects of Scottie? How? You must give specific examples for each element that you discuss. Your analysis may make reference to the film as a whole but should focus on the specific scenes.

SCENE 1

_____
_____
_____
_____
_____
_____
_____
_____
_____

_____
_____
_____
_____
_____
_____
_____
_____
_____

_____
_____
_____
_____
_____
_____
_____
_____

_____
_____
_____
_____
_____
_____
_____
_____

SCENE 2

_____

_____

_____

_____

_____

_____

_____

_____

_____

_____

_____

_____

_____

_____

_____

_____

_____

_____

_____

_____

_____

_____

_____

_____

_____

_____

_____

_____

_____